Understanding the Boys

Issues of Behaviour and Achievement

John Head

London and New York

First published 1999
by Falmer Press
11 New Fetter Lane, London EC4P 4EE

Simultaneously published in the USA and Canada
by Falmer Press
Routledge Inc, 29 West 35th Street, New York, NY 10001

Falmer Press is an imprint of the Taylor & Francis Group

© 1999 John Head

Typeset in Times by Falmer Press
Printed and bound in Great Britain by Biddles Ltd, Guildford and
King's Lynn

All rights reserved. No part of this book may be reprinted or
reproduced or utilized in any form or by any electronic,
mechanical, or other means, now known or hereafter
invented, including photocopying and recording, or in any
information storage or retrieval system, without permission in
writing from the publishers.

British Library Cataloguing in Publication Data
A catalogue record for this book is available from the British Library

Library of Congress Cataloguing in Publication Data
Understanding the boys: issues of behaviour and achievement. John
Head. Includes bibliographical references and index.
1. Teenage boys – Education – Great Britain. 2. Teenage boys – Great
Britain – Psychology. 3. Teenage boys – Great Britain – Physiology. 4.
Academic achievement – Great Britain. 5. Teenage boys – Great
Britain – Social conditions. I. Title.
LC1390.H43 1999   99–28099
373.18235'1–dc21   CIP

ISBN 0–750–70867–0 (hbk)
ISBN 0–750–70866–2 (pbk)

Contents

Acknowledgements

I have worked for more than twenty years on some aspects of gender and education, initially focused on the low participation of girls in mathematics, science and technology. Within that time I have worked with numerous schools and colleagues, too many to list here, and my thanks are due to many. Additionally, I have been involved in relevant projects abroad, particularly in Denmark and Spain. More recently the emphasis has been on the underachievement of boys, and I am particularly grateful to the dozens of teachers with whom I have conducted in-service work. Although it is our responsibility within universities to handle theoretical ideas I believe that ultimately the test of our efforts lies in their applicability to practice, and we need a dialogue with serving teachers to ensure that purpose.

Throughout this time I have had the advice and support of an informal Gender Research Group at King's College and my thanks are due to all who have attended, and particularly to Jan Harding who set it up initially. I would like to list those who have worked in a sub-group, dealing with the issues of boys education: Jan Bigg, David Jackson, Helen Lucey, Sheila Macrae, Meg Maguire, Rob Pattman, Simon Pratt, Diane Reay, Jonathan Salisbury, Chris Shelley and Ian Wake.

I owe a particular debt to Simon Pratt, of North London University, for his comments on a draft of this book text.

Part I
Identifying the Issues

1   Introduction and Overview

For centuries, and in various cultures, young men have been seen as a focus for social concern. References to the rebelliousness and unconcern of youth can be found from the times of Classical Greece through to the descriptions of Teddy Boys, Rockers, Mods, Punks and such in the second half of the twentieth century. This youthful turbulence cut across class barriers, so that in 1517 a riot among apprentices in London led to 300 arrests and one death, while there were also riots in prestigious schools, such as Rugby in 1797 and at Winchester in 1793 and 1818. In the latter year it had to be put down by the military.

There was, however, the underlying belief that this phase in life, in which 'boys will be boys', will be followed by a time of maturation, in which the young men assume responsibilities of adult life. Adolescence was seen to provide a carefree interlude before entering these adult responsibilities. For example, Shakespeare in his Henry IV plays shows the evolution of Prince Hal, the future Henry V, from a drunken companion of Falstaff to a wise, mature monarch. Upon becoming king he forsakes the company of Falstaff. The defining moment is when the new king meets the Lord Justice, who had previously punished him for his misdemeanours. Initially Henry is hostile, but then demonstrates his new maturity, saying:

> You did commit me
> For which, I do commit into your hand
> The unstained sword that you have used to bear;
> With this remembrance, that you use the same
> With the like bold, just and impartial spirit
> As you have done 'gainst me. There is my hand.
> You shall be as a father to my youth.
> (*Henry IV, Part 2*: Act 5, scene 2, ll. 112–18)

What is new is that some contemporary youth seems unable to shake off this time of adolescent rebellion and instability. We have long had evidence that the boys lagged behind girls in some respects, for example in the former

11 plus examinations, but it was assumed that the later maturing boys would eventually catch up and even overtake the girls, and the greater participation of males in higher education seemed to confirm this belief. More recently there has been less evidence of boys catching up in this way.

For several decades up until the early 1990s considerable attention was given to this gender inequality in education, manifested by the lack of women in higher education. This educational deficit was seen to be a major causal factor for the finding that on average women's wages were less than 80 per cent than those of men. Like many educationists at that time, I was involved in a number of research and curriculum development initiatives aimed at increasing the participation of girls, particularly in mathematics, science and technology, where traditionally boys had predominated. Although in these subjects males still seem advantaged at the post-16 level, the evidence is that some real progress was made in working towards greater equity.

It was in the mid-1990s that a new element was introduced into the debates about gender: that across a range of educational indices boys were emerging as the underachievers. This argument was found both in the academic research literature and the public media. Typical headlines have included: 'Girls trounce the boys in examination league tables' (*The Times*, 3 Sept. 1994) and have continued since then with: 'Perils of ignoring our lost boys' (*The Times Educational Supplement*, 28 June 1996), 'Time we had jobs for the boys' (*Daily Telegraph*, 5 Jan. 1998) and 'Grim reading for males' (*Guardian*, 6 Jan. 1998). In a major speech in January 1998 the then schools minister, Stephen Byers, drew attention to some salient evidence, such as that boys make up 83 per cent of school pupils who are permanently excluded from schools, and went on to make an attack on what he described as the prevailing 'laddish anti-learning culture'. Summing up the evidence in an article in *The Times Educational Supplement* (16 May 1997) Professor Ted Wragg warned 'unless we improve significantly the achievement of boys in our society now, we are storing up immense problems for the whole of the 21st century'. Clearly something significant has entered the public consciousness.

In 1996 the Equal Opportunities Commission and the Office for Standards in Education produced a joint report on performance differences between boys and girls in school (EOC/OFSTED, 1996). Their findings include 'Girls are more successful than boys ... or broadly as successful in almost all major subjects ... the only major subject in which girls perform significantly less well than boys was GCSE physics' (p. 6). They report that girls tend to be more reflective than boys and also better at planning and organising their work (p. 17).

Reactions to these findings that boys are doing less well in school and are also suffering in other respects, such as a disproportionate degree of unemployment, have varied. Some have identified what they see to be a crucial social problem of our time. Others see it as solely a symptom of a male backlash, creating a sense of moral panic, aimed at clawing back the gains made by women in recent years. In the light of such diverse views we need to maintain a sense of balance, scrutinize the evidence with care and seek practical ways to alleviate any problems which can be identified.

Looking at the Evidence

Looking at academic achievement first, we find that the most commonly quoted data relates to the GCSE results of 16-year-old school students. Over the years both boys and girls have raised their performance, but the girls have increased their advantage. In 1991 40.3 per cent of the girls and 33.3 per cent of the boys gained five or more passes with A to C grades. By 1996 50.2 per cent of the girls and 41.2 per cent of the boys attained such a result. It can be seen that both genders have raised their levels of achievement in this period but the gap between the them has increased. Prior to the introduction of the GCSE examination the gap was smaller, being only 4 per cent for the equivalent examination grades in 1988. This finding led to the government intervening in 1994 to force the examination boards to reduce the weighting given to course work in the overall examination grades on the basis that boys were less successful with the routines of course work. As the figures show, this intervention did nothing to close the gap.

Throughout this period girls have done better in the humanities and language-based subjects, but the figures for the two genders have diverged, so that in 1996 40.1 per cent of the boys and 57.7 per cent of the girls gained an A to C grade in English. With the traditional male subjects, such as science and mathematics, the figures have converged, with the girls catching up and, in most cases, overtaking the boys. The figures for 1996 show 40.9 per cent of the girls gaining A to C grades in mathematics compared with 39.7 per cent for the boys, while 42.7 per cent of the girls and 41.4 per cent of the boys gain such a grade in at least one science subject.

All the percentages quoted in the previous two paragraphs come from the DfEE (1997) publication of statistics and quote passes as a percentage of the total year cohort in schools. Sometimes other measures are quoted, for example the pass rates for those entering the examination in a particular subject. In most cases the differences between the two ways of presenting the information are trivial, but in some instances might cause confusion. In 1996 the participation rates for chemistry were 7.0 per cent for boys and 4.7 per cent for girls while 6.2 per cent of the boys and 4.2 per cent of the girls in the year gained A to C grades. In other words girls had a better pass rate but lower participation rate, and the final outcome came from the interaction of these two variables and, in this instance, the latter had the greater effect.

With post-16 education we find a similar pattern of girls doing relatively better but here they start from a historically poorer base. In 1995 girls made up 52 per cent of the entries for the GCE A level examinations at the age of

18 and they achieved a slightly better pass rate, for example 53.9 per cent gaining A to C grades compared to 53.0 per cent for the boys. At about the same time women became a majority among university undergraduates, although the difference as yet amounts to less than 2 per cent. Among undergraduates there are immense differences between subjects so that women are in a clear majority in the humanities, language areas, law and education but comprise considerably less than 40 per cent in the physical sciences, computer science and engineering areas.

It is difficult to predict precisely what the long-term effects of this increased success of girls will be. Currently there is the paradox that, despite this story of success, the average earnings for women still lag at about 20 per cent behind those of men. A number of factors may contribute to this situation. There will be a time-lag. Many of our current wage-earners left school two or three decades ago, at a time when girls did not compete so well. In this event we can predict a steady reduction of this earnings gap as more well qualified women enter the labour market. There are other variables. Often the family dynamics are such that the career interests of the husband are given greater priority than those of the wife so the family may move to allow the man to take on a better job but will not do so for the woman. If this latter effect prevails then women will continue to earn less than men.

In the light of such complexities we might not worry too much if these records of academic achievement were the only concern we have about boys. It might be argued that academic success is not essential to a happy life or gainful employment. However, there is further evidence of a male malaise. In 1997 the overall unemployment rates for males were 8.1 per cent for men and 5.8 per cent for women (Office for National Statistics, 1998). With men aged 16–19 the rate was 18.2 per cent and for those aged 20 to 24 it was 14.0 per cent. These two cohorts suffered from the two highest unemployment rates among the total population. Other indices tell a similar story. Overall suicide rates have dropped in the last two or three decades, but between 1971 and 1992 they more than doubled for males aged 16–24 and also increased by about two-thirds for males aged 25–44. One further piece of evidence is that of the crime figures, which show that to a large extent crime is an activity of young men with about 9 per cent of the 18–20 year olds being cautioned or found guilty of an indictable offence. For men aged over 30 years the figure is under 2 per cent.

Taking all this evidence into consideration, that of academic underachievement, school exclusion, unemployment, suicides and crime, there can be no doubt that there is some contemporary problem with young men which needs to be addressed. In saying this, I have no wish to deny that in a number of respects women are still disadvantaged in our society and we should rejoice at the academic success of girls in recent years. The task is not to deny the successes of women but to see what is needed to improve the lot of the young men.

Issues in Context

One factor which has inhibited us understanding what is happening to contemporary youth is that we tend to see each symptom as a discrete matter, without exploring the context and causes. In undertaking in-service work with teachers I find many Heads of Department asking for tips for improving the GCSE performances in their own subject without asking about the overall story. We find a range of professional people, such as teachers, educational psychologists, probation officers and youth workers, all concerned about the behaviour of young men, but not commonly sharing their professional insights.

Too often simplistic analysis is made from one specific perspective. Sometimes it is that of biological determinism, such as someone recently commenting on television that all men were rapists as their behaviour was dictated by the effects of the hormone testosterone. Is this statement meant to be taken literally? It is difficult to sustain a biological argument for the finding that rape is much more common in certain American urban areas than in the South East Asian cities. Probably a combination of effective policing and social mores contribute to this variance. Examples of youth engaging in gang rape indicate that participation does not damage the individual in the sight of his male peers, it may enhance his status in making him seem macho. In other societies being guilty of rape would bring shame to the family and condemnation from peers.

It is equally easy to find examples of simplistic social determinism, such as in the statement that poverty produces crime. There is an association, with about half our criminal families coming from the lowest fifth of the social economic spectrum. But it is also true that the majority of the families within this social stratum are not criminal. Social factors do matter, for example unemployment rates among young men vary with location, social class and ethnicity, but the relationship is subtle and complex.

The third background factor likely to affect behaviour lies in the personal history of the individual. Sometimes too much significance is attributed to early personal history, with people taking from psycho-analysis the mistaken belief that their life is solely determined by their past so that they are doomed to a certain lifestyle. They do not recognize their capacity to think, make decisions and shape their own life. Nevertheless, personal experience will be one of the factors shaping behaviour and needs to be considered alongside the biological and social contributions.

Any comprehensive understanding must incorporate all the elements shown in Figure 1 (on p. 8). Biological, social and personal history all affect individuals, but they still have the capacity to be reflexive and to make decisions about matters such as their career and lifestyle.

BIOLOGICAL EFFECTS ↘

PERSONAL HISTORY ⇢   MENTAL PROCESSES ⇢ OUTCOMES

SOCIAL FACTORS ↗

Figure 1.1   Underlying causes of behaviour

The importance of mental process is that it represents the one place in which we can make an intervention. We cannot rewrite history and alter the social background and personal experience of the individual. What can be done is to help people recognize that there are options open to them so that they can take more control of their life. By making young people aware of options and causing them to consider possibilities we can most effectively address the current male malaise. The structure of this book is intended to reflect this causal model. In Part I the underlying causes of any male malaise are explored and in Part II the emphasis is on the outcomes and what practical steps can be taken to address the issues.

Generalizations and Diversity

Already in this text warnings have been given about the validity of generalizations and the need to scrutinize evidence with care. In writing this book I have the problem that almost on every page I ought to repeat this warning. Unfortunately, this practice would make dull reading. At various places the problems of some specific groups, are discussed, such as white working-class boys, Afro-Caribbean boys and those suffering from dyslexia. Much of the time generalizations are made without qualification and it is hoped that we do not lose sight of the diversity which exists among young men and boys. Some display academic underachievement and behavioural difficulties, but many do not. In focusing on the former we should not lose sight of the latter.

2   Biological Effects

A model which sees biology as the underlying cause of human behaviour has appeal for its clarity and simplicity. With very rare exceptions children can be identified by their biological sex at birth and all subsequent development can then be attributed to the unfolding of a plan contained in the genes. Unfortunately, the reality proves to be much more complicated and confusing.

Clearly some of the characteristics which distinguish men from women, such as the style of dress and length of hair, are simply matters of social custom. Young men in the 1960s and 1970s commonly wore their hair in a style which would have appeared effete twenty years earlier or later. In order to clarify the issues it has become a convention to distinguish between sex differences and gender differences, with the former referring to the biological and the latter to the social. The ability to give birth to children and breast-feed them is solely biological, a characteristic of one sex, while other differences are attributed to the social. Even this distinction is not clear cut. Child bearing can only be undertaken by females while child rearing could be undertaken by either sex. Consequently the fact that women usually take the major role in child rearing is a gender difference, yet it has some biological basis, in that the mother may have to be with the child in order to feed it. Similarly, there is some biological sense in asking men to undertake work which involves physical endeavour, as they tend to enjoy greater muscular development, even though at times of war, when men are away from home, the female population have coped very effectively in factories and on farms with traditional male work.

It is easy to see why Freud opted for a biological basis for his notions of psychology. When he started his original work at the beginning of the twentieth century, psychology was subject to a confusing mix of influences. Ideas were rooted in such diverse sources as neurology, moral philosophy and theology so, for example, human behaviour was explained in terms of Original Sin with humans being seen as fallen angels. Freud sought to establish a coherent, secular and rational psychology and the only discipline he had at hand to provide an intellectual base was that of biology. In our postmodernist age his work can be seen to be over-ambitious, yet despite the many flaws which have become apparent we should recognize both the intellectual achievement his work represented and the many valid insights he provided.

A more contemporary biological determinist perspective comes from sociobiology, a discipline which marries studies of animal behaviour with the concept of evolution. It is argued that human behaviour today is simply the product of an evolutionary process, so that perceived gender differences in our culture are simply rooted in biological sex differences. Even within its own terms this explanation is not plausible. Evolutionary modification and development is a slow process in which, as the external conditions change, some individuals prove to be advantaged and, by reproducing themselves more effectively, edge out others. But too much of our social change has occurred too quickly for this mechanism to come into operation. In a typical life span of about seventy years, starting from 1930, the population has had to adapt to new ways of living, ranging from jet travel to living in a centrally heated environment to eating microwaved foods. Go back 200 years and we find a people without cars and trains, having no gas or electricity, largely leading a rural life. The capacity of humans to cope with such rapid changes reflects more a capacity to learn, and less a process of natural selection leading to changes being established in successive generations.

We may wish to challenge the idea of biological *causes* of behaviour, but that does not deny biological *influences*. Arthur Koestler in *The Ghost in the Machine* (1967) suggested that humans carry within them some inherited characteristics which put them at risk in coping with contemporary society. In particular, he argued that humans are unusual among animals in killing members of their own species. When people only had their own strength and primitive weapons this characteristic may not have been too damaging. When people have access to a technology which provides weapons of mass destruction this trait could threaten all mankind. I am not specifically advocating Koestler's views here, but am using them to demonstrate what might be the limit of biological influences, a tendency to behave in particular ways. This tendency still remains subject to the control of conscious minds.

It might be useful at this stage to draw the distinction between behaviour which comes from instinct and that which is learnt. An analogy can be made between that which is built into the hardware of the computer, correspond-ing to the instincts, and the learnt behaviour which is closer to the software. Animals, particularly the more primitive, are largely governed by their instincts. This inborn capacity has advantages. For example, when a turtle hatches from the sand it does not need an adult to guide it to the sea, it instinctively proceeds down the beach and into the water. The drawback of instinctive behaviour is its inflexibility, so that species might not adapt well to changing circumstances.

Humans are born with very limited instinctive powers and are consequently totally helpless in their infancy, needing adults to ensure their survival. What humans possess, by virtue of their large brain, is the capacity to learn, so they not only learn the skills common to other animals, such as walking, but many more, such as speech. Because humans are less dependent on the 'hard-wiring' of the brain they have the capacity to adapt relatively easily to changing circumstances. It is therefore likely that, to a large extent, gender differences are also largely learnt after birth, although this statement does not deny the possible existence of a residual biological factor, Koestler's *Ghost in the Machine*. Human babies do display some instinctive behaviour, to feed from a breast and pay attention to faces, but overwhelmingly adult behaviour seems to be dominated by what has been learnt.

Further difficulties associated with biological explanations emerge when we try to ascertain what is the crucial biological distinction between the two sexes.

Males and Females

Anatomy

Freud, for example, had no doubt that the anatomical differences in the genitalia determined the subsequent psychological development of the person. He assumed that at a very early age children were aware of the anatomical differences between men and women. For the boy the possession of a penis gave him a sense of power and desire for women, initially directed towards his mother (the Oedipus complex), which subsequently was countered by a fear of castration by his rival, his own father. The ensuing castration complex laid the foundation for the boy to develop a sense of morality. The girl felt herself as being incomplete compared to a boy (penis envy) and had to reconcile herself to a relatively passive role until eventually she would be courted by a man.

It is easy to identify a series of objections to this theory, which would only be accepted in its entirety today by committed Freudians. It is by no means clear that children are fully aware of the anatomical differences. Many boys grow up in the absence of a father so may not develop a castration complex. Not surprisingly, feminists have criticized a model which effectively relegates women to a secondary status as being incomplete men.

Although most of us would be critical of Freud we often implicitly accept his belief that 'anatomy is destiny'. The first things we are told about a child are that it is healthy and its sex. Apart from anything else, we need to know the sex in order to select the appropriate personal pronouns, such as he or she, in talking about the child. From this point onwards, in ways which will be elaborated in the next chapter, by the ways we treat the child, the biological sex is taken as the key distinguishing characteristic.

It is only in some exceptional circumstances that the basis of this belief is revealed as being uncertain. When transsexuals undergo surgery to change their sex they may wish to have the description on their birth certificate altered. In most countries such a change cannot be made. It is argued that the genitalia are not, after all, really the determining characteristic. The clearest example of this stance is in relation to athletics. Competitors in the 1964 Olympics were confirmed as being female on the basis of visual inspection. Subsequently, it was realized that a mix of hormone treatment and surgery might cause men to be entered in competitions as women, and the type of sex chromosomes was taken to be the crucial determinant. One of the 1964 medal winners was then judged to be male. It would seem, therefore, that we should look to the chromosomal make-up, rather than anatomy, for the biological basis of sex differences.

Chromosomes

All human cells, other than the gametes (ova and sperm), contain pairs of chromosomes, with one pair being specially associated with sex differences. Females possess two identical sex chromosomes, labelled as XX, while males contain a dissimilar pair, XY. Gametes only carry a single chromosome. As a woman only carries X cells, all the ova she produces must contain that chromosome. Each sperm cell contains either an X or a Y chromosome and consequently the sex of a child is usually determined by the nature of the sperm which fertilized the ovum. This description seems simple and clear, but once again closer scrutiny reveals complications.

There are a number of aberrations. Some people only possess a single sex chromosome, one X, and they develop to be infertile females, with a condition known as Turner's Syndrome. Others, who appear to be normal males, are found to have three sex chromosomes, either XXY or XYY. The XXY people have both a complete set for being female and a complete set for being male, yet do not usually display hermaphroditism, homosexuality or androgyny. The causal function of the chromosome pattern is not clear. All we can conclude is that a foetus needs at least one X chromosome to be viable, as children are not known to possess simply the Y chromosome, and that the presence of the Y chromosome nearly always gives rise to a male body.

There are further complications. For the first six weeks the foetus has an undifferentiated genitalia, with the potential to develop either way. Usually with a boy the hormone testosterone is then released, which causes this body material to develop with the typical male genitalia. Occasionally, for reasons which are not fully known, the foetus material is somewhat insensitive to the presence of the testosterone, so the body development occurs as if this hormone was not present. In this situation a child is born who has the chromosomes of a male and genitalia which may be intermediate (hermaphroditism) or seem like those of a female. It can also be the case that a metabolic disturbance causes a foetus carrying the XX chromosomes to be subjected to a high level of testosterone, so the child has female chromosomes but male external genitalia. The key question in these events is what wins out. Which is more important, the chromosomal pattern or the appearance of the external genitalia? This issue has been extensively studied (e.g. Money and Ehrhardt, 1972) and the surprising answer is that neither seem as important as the self-image of the child. Children born with this unusual body configuration have been brought up both as boys and as girls, according to the wishes of the parents and what seems to be anatomically the closer fit. Remedial surgery may be undertaken and then the child is brought up unambiguously within a conventional sex role. The crucial finding from the research is that these children seem to be equally happy regardless of the way they were identified. This finding denies the hypothesis that the sex chromosomes are somehow the crucial determinant.

Hormones

The next possibility in the search for the Holy Grail of an unambiguous biological root to gender is to consider the influence of hormones. Undoubtedly these substances do affect mood and behaviour, as most clearly shown during pregnancy and in the condition of pre-menstrual tension. It is also true that, although males and females produce the same hormones, the relative abundance varies, with men producing more androgens, in particular testosterone, while women produce more of the oestrogens. It might seem logical to suggest that observed differences simply arise from these hormonal differences. Specifically, it is often suggested that male aggression comes from the influence of testosterone.

There is a link between testosterone secretion and aggression, but it is not the one that is usually postulated. Clear evidence with rhesus monkeys show that after a male has been in a fight, and emerged as the victor, testosterone levels rise, and this then enhances their libido (Rose et al., 1972). Presumably this is an evolutionary effect, ensuring that the strongest males are most likely to father offspring. Travis and Wade (1984) have shown that with men one consequence of depression is a lowered level of testosterone release. From such studies we learn that we must reject the simple idea that testosterone causes aggression and adopt the more complicated belief that a sense of well-being, which follows success, tends to stimulate the production of this hormone.

Brain Structure and Function

The last possibility for biological causation of gender differences is that boys and girls are born with some in-built differences in their brains. Men tend to have larger brains and this fact was used in the nineteenth century to justify the exclusion of women from higher education. The contemporary belief is that intellectual capacity is more related to the complexity of the interconnections between the brain cells, or neurones (alternative spelling, neuron), rather than to the size of the brain, or the number of neurones in the brain, and there is no evidence of a major sex difference.

There have been consistent reports of gender differences, with girls being better in the language areas, learning to speak, read and write at an earlier age than boys. Boys do relatively well at science and mathematics. These findings have led to suggestions that there is a sex difference in brain structure. Underlying this notion is the belief that mental functions can be mapped onto the areas of the brain. Such one-to-one correspondence does exist with some processes, particularly motor functions, so areas can be identified in the brain which control, for example, one hand or part of the face. If a region of the brain is damaged there will be a corresponding loss of sensation and muscle control in the appropriate part of the body.

However, higher mental functions, such as those largely acquired through learning, do not map onto the brain this way. Memories are not encoded on a digital basis on individual neurones, but are stored on a connected set of several thousand neurones. Long filaments, or dendrites, make up these connections and they allow the storage of a particular memory to be spread out over the whole brain. There are at least three advantages to this holistic way of storing knowledge. Neurones are continuously dying, so if a memory were stored on one single neurone there would be a great risk of it being totally lost. Someone might suddenly forget where they lived while on their way home from work. Second, the arrangement allows faster access to stored knowledge. A brain contains about 20 billion neurones, so however fast the scanning mechanism might be, there would be long delays while attempting to retrieve the knowledge. Having storage on 10,000 neurones speeds up the process by this factor. It is a controversial question within psychology whether memories are ever lost or if retrieval presents the challenge. We all have experienced the situation in which we suddenly recall something which we had not previously realized we had remembered. The final advantage is that a system of storage on a combination of neurones from within the large total confers an immense increase in the potential capacity of the brain to store knowledge.

Going back to the finding that girls do better at languages and boys at science and mathematics we can see that even if brain function is a causal factor there still remain two possibilities for the origin of the sex difference. One hypothesis is that boys and girls are born with different brains. The other possibility is that different skills develop through different experiences and use of the brain. This latter possibility is consistent with our knowledge about the brain functions. Most brain growth occurs early in life. If the brain is not fully used then some of its functions literally atrophy; the neurones do not connect up with each other. If, in other cases, an experience is repeated, so that it becomes a routine, strong neural pathways are established, so that the operation becomes easier. A learner driver may find the series of activities involved in changing gear to be a challenge. An experienced driver can change gear without thinking much about it, while simultaneously watching the road and talking to a passenger. It is therefore possible that boys and girls develop different intellectual skills through having different experiences and establishing different routines. As we will see in the next chapter there is strong evidence that this process is a causal factor for gender differences.

The final biological argument is that perceived cognitive differences may arise because males and females differ in which hemisphere of the brain is more dominant. Again a simple hypothesis presents difficulties. On the one hand men might be seen to be more right hemisphere dominant, as suggested by their better visual-spatial skills, but, equally, they can also be seen to be more left dominant by virtue of their mathematical skills and powers of logical reasoning. In the face of such evidence the notion of brain hemisphere dominance does little to account for gender differences. The only gender difference which has emerged from brain research is that brain function seems to be more localized among males, while females use more of the brain to address a given task; but in itself this finding explains little. Advocates of biological causation of gender differences in learning, for example Moir and Moir (1998), argue that girls are better at language tasks as they are more able to use both hemispheres and use more brain power. But they argue that the superiority of boys with mathematical and spatial tasks is because they only use one hemisphere and thus avoid the confusion which arises when both hemispheres are involved in a cognitive task. The contradiction in these arguments seems to be ignored in the wish to get a theory to fit the facts.

The Vulnerable Male

Looking at young men performing on the sports field, walking down the street with a characteristic strut, or sprawled at ease in an armchair with limbs spread out claiming much of the space in the room, we believe that we are seeing the epitome of physical health and strength. Against this background it is difficult to realize that in many essentials males are biologically the vulnerable sex.

One obvious line of evidence is that of life expectancies, seventy-four years and four months for men and seventy-nine years and seven months for women. Ninety-five years earlier the figures were forty-five years and five months for men and forty-nine years for women. The improvements in diet, living conditions and medical care in the twentieth century have clearly conferred immense advantages to all, yet the gender differential has scarcely changed. Remembering that many women have had to undergo the physical strain of child bearing, this discrepancy is surprising.

The roots of this difference, the sites of male vulnerability, lie at the other end of the life-span, starting with the foetus. Far more boys than girls are conceived. The explanation for this difference is believed to be that the Y carrying sperm is much lighter and more mobile than that carrying an X chromosome, so is more effective in reaching and fertilizing the ovum. The estimates vary somewhat, but are in the range of 20–30 per cent more boys being conceived. However, the male foetus develops more slowly, and is more vulnerable to miscarriage, so that in the past fewer boys were born, and fewer still survived infancy. Improved ante-natal and paediatric care has altered the balance so that currently boys are in excess among children by about 2 per cent. This alteration in the ratio between the sexes raises new demographic and social issues which will be discussed in Chapter 6 of this book.

Part of this vulnerability of the young male comes from his relatively slow development, so that boys are on most measures about four weeks less mature at birth than girls who have experienced the same span of pregnancy. It must be remembered that the genetic plan for human development is for a foetus to develop into the female, and for a boy to be produced that plan has to be altered under the influence of the Y chromosome and subsequent hormonal changes. This process, of switching the foetus on to the male track, seems to interfere with and delay development. Once born, males are more vulnerable to a range of physical and mental disorders. Some of these probably occur through the immaturity of the boys, so that normal span male births resemble in some respects the vulnerability of the premature child, while other disorders arise from a specific genetic condition, commonly known as the *fragile-X syndrome*.

The smaller Y chromosome mainly acts to switch foetal development onto the male path. The larger X chromosome has less to do in relation to sexual development and instead encodes information relating to a wide range of developmental factors. It is also true that the X chromosome seems unusually prone to damage or mutation so that it carries information which can produce physical disorders. In the case of a girl she has two X chromosomes, and provided one of them is intact she does not suffer from the disorder. The intact chromosome will dominate while the other is described as *recessive* and has no obvious effect on the girl. The boy only carries one X chromosome so if that is damaged he will experience the disorder. Genetically controlled conditions, linked to the X chromosome in this way, include the commonest form of colour-blindness, haemophilia and muscular dystrophy.

Women who carry a damaged X gene will be a carriers and statistically half their sons will inherit the disorder, while half their daughters will, in turn, be carriers. The daughters of a male haemophiliac will all be carriers, as he only has one X chromosome to pass on to them, while none of his sons will suffer, as he contributed a Y chromosome to their conception. Notionally, females can experience the same physical disorder if both their

X chromosomes are damaged. Thus with a mild disorder, such as red-green colour blindness, about 1 male in 20 suffers to some degree and about 1 female in 400. With the less common, but more severe conditions, the females seem to suffer less than statistics might predict, possibly because the carrying of two defective chromosomes causes the foetus to be aborted.

In the instances discussed the role of the damaged X chromosome has been clearly established. What is less clear is the possible influence it has on a wider range of conditions. Boys are more vulnerable to infection and a wide range of diseases. They are also far more vulnerable to problems with some mental functions, as seen in autism or dyslexia. Whether these conditions have a genetic origin remains uncertain, but, whatever the explanation, we find a majority of boys among those in paediatric care and with Special Needs provision within the educational service.

The slow maturation of boys continues up to puberty, which girls reach about eighteen months earlier than boys. The increased vulnerability to illness affects the demographic balance, so currently males are in a majority among the population under the age of about 40 while females are in a majority among older people.

Seen in this context, the vigour of male youth conceals an inner vulnerability, and tends to prove to be a short-lived advantage.

The Male and his Body

Hitherto in this chapter we have been concentrating on one aspect of the mind–body duality, that of the possible biological influences on the development and behaviour of males. In this last section it is intended to consider the reverse process, looking at how men perceive and treat their body.

There are some striking gender differences. The widespread belief that women are more self-conscious and concerned about their body-image is confirmed by empirical evidence (Fisher, 1973; Grogan, 1998). Men tend to separate more clearly the mind from the body and adopt a distancing process in regarding their body. This mechanism confers some advantages: it can help with the experience of moderate pain, so that the athlete may notice discomfort but is able to attribute it to part of the body and not let it impinge too much on the core mental processes. Among young men it is 'cool' to be able to shrug off injuries gained through sports and fights. Interestingly, drugs such as morphine have a similar effect, such that one is aware of pain but is able to cope with it. The negative side of this mental process of separation is that men may cease to take care of their body, either in terms of appearance or of seeking help with symptoms of illness. For example, men often leave it for a long time before reporting the characteristic signs of heart conditions and peptic ulcers.

One outcome of this male neglect of the body is that ailments which specifically affect men are not prioritized in medicine. About 12,000 men die in Britain of prostate cancer each year, nearly the same as the number of women who die of breast cancer. There is no screening programme for prostate cancer, even though a simple blood test is fairly accurate. Additionally, there is widespread uncertainty about the factors which control the speed of development of these cancers and of the best procedures for treatment. It might be thought that such ignorance would inspire an extensive research effort but often the condition is simply dismissed as a natural consequence of men ageing.

No such argument can be employed with testicular cancer, which is a killer of young men. In this case simple self-examination should provide early diagnosis but most young men are totally unaware of the need and procedure. There seems to be a resistance among such men, and even those involved in health promotion, in talking about a process which might be interpreted as a morbid interest in one's own genitalia. About 1,400 cases of testicular cancer are identified in this country each year. If found at an early stage, while the condition is still localized, the prognosis is very favourable with a recovery rate in excess of 95 per cent. However, in nearly half the cases the cancer has been allowed to develop so that it has invaded other parts of the body. In these cases the mortality rate is increased ten-fold so that over 300 young men die unnecessarily each year.

The final taboo in talking about the male body relates to impotence. Recent publicity, largely driven by the introduction of the drug Viagra, has led to help-lines receiving literally thousands of calls. The vast majority of callers have never previously sought help but suffered in silence. Although the condition is more common with older men, it is believed to affect about 8 per cent of those aged under 35 years.

Possibly we are currently experiencing some social change in respect to these issues. One aspect of the consumerist society has been the increased attention to men's appearance, in relation to both clothes and personal grooming. Similarly, the existence of a magazine called *Men's Health* on the bookstalls, suggests changing attitudes. What is not yet clear is to what extent we are witnessing a widespread change in attitudes across the greater part of the population or whether it is simply a replay of the eighteenth-century fop, with a small privileged sector of society paying attention to the condition of men.

Another factor reported by Fisher is that men have a stronger sense of body-boundary:

> the average woman feels more secure about her body boundaries than does the average man ... men are more disturbed when they get the feeling that something has bypassed their body boundaries and gained access to their interior.

(1973: 44–5)

Possibly this fear partly accounts for the reluctance of men to seek medical help and the widely reported resistance of men to receiving an injection with a hypodermic syringe.

Fisher suggests that in this instance biological sex differences may be involved. If women are to undergo conventional sexual intercourse then they have to experience penetration of their body, so they recognize that such penetration need not be unpleasant or threatening. Erik Erikson (1968), the leading post-Freudian theorist of adolescence, suggested that girls develop a sense of 'inner space'. Observing 300 children aged 10–12 years playing with toys, he noticed that girls tended to build open structures, such as a room, and models of animals or humans were placed within the room. Boys used toys in more dynamic ways, moving objects around in such a fashion that objects collided and structures were knocked down.

Erikson drew two conclusions from these observations. The first was to postulate that these differences in play reflected different self-images of the body, which may be true. Second, he shifted from the descriptive to the prescriptive in suggesting that women ought to be more passive and men the more active in their adult life. Essentially, he saw women having a restricted range of choices in life while waiting for the right man to arrive and marry them. Like Freud, Erikson was in some respects trapped in the mind-set of his time. As I will argue later in Chapter 6, in the contemporary situation it is women who have the greater range of options in their life.

What does emerge from this section is that the lack of ease of young men in talking about their bodies and health makes it more difficult for those working in social, personal and health education to provide an effective service. The overcoming of such resistance to thought and discussion is part of the agenda which will be discussed in later chapters.

3 Personal History

Childhood and Adolescence

In the first half of the twentieth century there was a division of opinion about child care. One school of thought believed that once the child's material needs had been met then no more needed to be done. Constantly paying attention to a child, for example picking it up when it cried, tended to spoil the infant who would be making ever increasing demands for attention. Others, including those influenced by psychoanalysis, believed that interactions with adults played a crucial role in child development.

The argument was firmly settled in favour of the latter position through the work of John Bowlby. Following a review of child rearing practices world-wide he produced an influential report for the World Health Organization (Bowlby, 1951). He had identified a number of orphanages in various countries in which infants were given proper care for their material needs, being fed and kept clean and warm, but received little other attention. Often they would be placed in cots with high sides so that they could see little apart from the ceiling. Such children revealed both social and intellectual retardation as they matured. Typically their speech was limited. They had difficulty in relating to both adults and other children, tending to withdraw into a quiet corner. It became increasingly clear that children need to be stimulated by talk, touch and play. Remembering that at birth the infant's brain is already half its adult size and will reach 90 per cent by the age of 5, it is not unreasonable to assume that vital cognitive development occurs in these years. Bowlby (1951) summed up his work with the words, 'mother love in infancy and childhood is as important for mental health as vitamins and proteins for physical health'.

This argument has become widely accepted, witness the attention paid to early learning, with the use of brightly coloured toys which can be manipulated to produce sounds or be joined together. What remains more controversial is the explanation for what actually matters within the child and adult interaction.

Attachment and Separation

For Freud the earliest factor came from the child's oral gratification, gained by feeding at its mother's breast, and for the first three years of life the relationship with the mother was seen to be central. In the next two years the developmental sequence followed by a boy meant that he had to overcome his Oedipus complex for his mother in order to identify with the father.

There are a number of objections to this model. The resolution of the Oedipus complex was regarded as setting up the dynamic tension between desire and constraint which characterized the adult personality. As girls would not experience the Oedipus complex Freud had no explanation for their development other than being stuck throughout childhood in the position of envying the boy. If Freud's description is true we might anticipate that males would be the more psychologically mature and stable, but in fact, the evidence largely supports the reverse position. Males tend to be less happy in their gender role, with a higher proportion being transsexual, and they are more prone to violence and more likely to be social misfits (Stoller, 1985). For these reasons there has been a search for an alternative model.

Bowlby was initially influenced by psychoanalysis, but increasingly the strictly Freudian view has yielded to the variant of psychoanalysis known as Object Relations theory, which was developed in different ways by Melanie Klein (1932), Fairbairn (1952) and Winnicott (1958). Object Relations theory tends to place less emphasis on the nature of a person in isolation and greater emphasis on the form of the significant relationships that person has with others. In this model the key fact is seen to be the helplessness of the infant, who is not a viable being unless it receives care and attention from others. Very early on the infant learns to recognize the face and voice of the primary caretaker, the person who is undertaking most of the care, and responds to that person. Usually the biological mother will be the primary caretaker, but it need not be so. This point marks the distinction with the Freudian view. Freud prioritized the biological link between the mother and child, reinforced by the experience of breast-feeding. Object Relations theory recognizes the central role of the primary caretaker in providing security for the infant, but any suitable adult, male or female, could fulfil this role.

This attachment between the child and the primary caretaker cannot continue forever. At some stage the child has to begin to separate him or herself in order to develop into an autonomous being. It is when we look at the early stages of this separation that it becomes apparent that little boys and girls tend to be treated differently.

Gender and Early Experience

Probably the most important account of this gender difference comes in the book *The Reproduction of Mothering* by Nancy Chodorow (1978). As its clever title indicates, she is suggesting that girls are socialized as children into becoming potential mothers, with this process of social reproduction being undertaken by mothers.

The essential point is that boys and girls have an asymmetric experience of childhood. For both, the primary caretaker is usually female. Boys learn to become men by being different from her while girls can learn to become a woman by identifying with her. Lynn (1962) and Greenson (1968) pointed out that in this case boys have the more difficult task, in having to change and dis-identify with the mother, while for girls there is no such abrupt change. The situation is roughly analogous with the physical development of the foetus in which the boys have to cope with a more complex and hazardous developmental sequence.

Mothers tend to treat boys as being different from themselves. Boys are allowed more autonomy and are encouraged to show characteristics which are deemed to be masculine, such as coping with the rough-and-tumble of play without crying. Girls are held closer to the mother and are brought into the role of a helper with stereotypical female tasks within the house, such as cleaning and cooking. More talk is directed to the girl, so she becomes initiated into the interests and concerns of the mother. It is this process which Chodorow saw as preparing girls for motherhood.

It is easy to observe these differences in the ways little boys and girls are treated but there has been disagreement about the causal processes. Sometimes it has been argued that the baby boys and girls are genetically programmed to elicit different responses from adults. Boys, it will be argued, will pursue independence while girls will seek care and protection. In this event the observed differences in parental care are driven by the actual biology of the child.

This hypothesis has been demonstrated to be untrue. One of the earlier and more important studies came from Smith and Lloyd (1978) who observed infants being cared for by various women in a child clinic. A mother had her own child removed for a medical check-up and was then asked to care for another unknown infant for a while. Sometimes the same infant was described as being a girl and at other times a boy as it was handed over to different women. It would not be easy to distinguish a clothed infant. If the baby cried and was believed to be a boy it was stimulated by being bounced up and down. If it was believed to be a girl it was caressed and comforted. Those seen to be a boy were allowed to crawl further around the room. Those believed to be a girl were talked to more. From this study it can be seen that the crucial factor is not the actual sex of the child but its perceived sex. Essentially, therefore, we are describing a social process rather than one which is biologically determined and this finding has received subsequent support (e.g. Culp et al., 1983).

The key fact is that boys in our culture are encouraged to gain autonomy earlier than girls. There seems to be a widespread fear that a boy will become a 'sissy' if held too close to the mother for too long. The danger for boys is that they may experience this separation too early for them to cope with it. The corresponding danger for girls is that they may have the separation delayed to the extent that they find it difficult to cope with autonomy as adults. It is beyond the scope of this book to pursue the story of female development, but the process by which adolescent girls have to re-negotiate their relationship with the mother can be found in Apter (1989).

Hudson and Jacot (1991) have coined the term 'the male wound' to describe what might come from this early separation of the boy. He may feel rejected by his mother and consequently distrust other people, particularly women, such that he becomes a misogynist. To avoid the pain of further enforced separation the boy may attempt to keep some emotional distance in his relationships and value his independence, and take pride in the fact that he does not need others.

The early close relationship with the mother, or other primary caretaker, involves the child identifying with her. The word *identifying*, which has roots in psychoanalysis, has quite a strong meaning. It involves recognizing a similarity or identity, that the child realizes that he might grow up to be like this adult, but it goes further in suggesting that the beliefs and mores of the adult are taken on and internalized by the child. In essence, even when the adult is not present the child behaves in accordance to what it is assumed the parent would say.

Obviously the extent of this male wound will depend on a number of variables, the timing, the extent the mother can prepare the boy for his new position, and the presence of a father figure with whom the boy can identify. In many cases this developmental hurdle may not present too much difficulty, but there is little doubt that often boys have been treated harshly. For example, Watkins (1993) gives an autobiographical account of being sent away to a boarding school at the age of seven. He was given no warning or preparation:

> I swear, that I thought that I was going to a party.... My father drove me to a house that I had never seen before.... 'Goodbye', my father said, and shook my hand.
>
> (1993: 1)

The bewilderment and sense of betrayal resulting from this experience might endanger the capacity of a boy to relate closely to others. One wonders, too, whether parents in such a situation appreciate the distress they are causing. This example, of being sent to a boarding school at the age of seven, may seem extreme, but for many boys within a particular social stratum within England boarding starts only two years later at the age of nine.

The male wound can be seen to be a normative developmental issue, one which all boys are likely to experience to a greater or lesser degree. However, there are some variants which can yield considerable difficulties.

One possibility is that a boy never ceases to identify with the mother. In an extreme case he might be transsexual, believing himself to be psychologically a female who is trapped within a male body. Certainly there is evidence that an unusually close relationship between a dominant mother and a son is associated with degrees of gender confusion for the boy. Another possibility is that a boy dis-identifies with the mother figure but does not then identify with a male. In this event he may find himself in an emotional limbo in which such identification which does occur might be with a cause or ideology. The celibate life of a priest may appeal to such a boy. An alternative would be for him to develop into the mystic loner typified by Lawrence of Arabia. Obviously the presence of a caring father figure can be vitally important to the psychological development of the boy. Usually this will be the biological father, but others, such as grandparents or uncles can provide the necessary role model. One of the current concerns about primary schools is that they often lack male staff whose presence might contribute to this developmental process.

Maternal Deprivation Reviewed

The findings of Bowlby received confirmation from many sources so that the issue of *maternal deprivation* captured the media headlines. Subsequently, there has been a reaction, e.g. Clarke and Clarke (1976) and Rutter (1972), which does not challenge the main thesis, about the importance of adults providing stimulus to the child, but modifies points of emphasis.

One problem is that some mothers have felt themselves to be made scapegoats, so that if the child grows up to be backward or anti-social then it is seen that the mother is at fault. The reality seems to be that very young children need a few familiar people to relate to, but once these relationships are in place the ideal setting is probably that of an extended family. Different people within this large group can meet the various needs of the child. and it is not necessary for the mother figure to carry the whole responsibility.

What happens if the single parent family is headed by the father? It is difficult to say, as the evidence is limited, but they seem to be quite successful. Possibly, though, we are not comparing like with like, as it may be the exceptional father who takes on this role. Presumably the psychodynamics will be closer to those more commonly found with a mother and daughter, with identification providing security to the child which may delay growing into adult independence.

The other question is whether early neglect of a child can be compensated for by later intervention. Can the retarded language, intellectual and social development be made up? One only has to visit schools for Special Needs children to see staff doing just this with some success. It is, however, a difficult task involving intensive teaching. It seems as if there is an age at which children can readily learn something and if appropriate development does not take place then, it will be more difficult later on.

What does emerge from all this work is the belief that young boys do have a particularly difficult developmental task which affects them as adults, so that:

> masculinity seems to have a permanently defensive flavour about it. ... Male identity becomes an accomplishment, which men strive to act out, but one which – perhaps paradoxically – is defined most clearly in the negative. Masculinity is the absence of femininity.
>
> (Edley and Wetherell, 1995: 46)

Latency: The Years of Social Reinforcement

Once the child has acquired the maturity to leave the family for long enough to attend school he enters a period of relative stability which lasts until puberty and the onset of adolescence. In this period little new occurs but the lessons learnt in childhood are continuously being reinforced.

Ask a boy aged three or four years about himself and the three things he is likely to tell you are his name, age and the fact that he is a boy. His gender is already seen as a source for his sense of identity.

Inside school his sense of gender differences will be continuously reinforced by comments of the form: 'Just like a boy' or 'Boys don't cry'. Boys and girls are given different toys and are encouraged to pursue different hobbies and play activities. It is noticeable that girls are allowed more variation than boys. The girl who is a tomboy may receive some grudging respect but the boy playing with dolls is likely to invite a reprimand in one form or another. Within the turmoil of coping with school, children tend to seek alliance with like companions. Given a free choice of companions to play with we find that at the age of four, children spend three-quarters of the time playing within single-sex groups and at the age of six and a half years they will be in single-sex groups for more than 90 per cent of the time (Maccoby and Jacklin, 1987). The single-sex groups develop their own rules and procedures, which control play and discourse, so that boys and girls find it difficult to communicate with each other. Girls will complain that boys are always being competitive and critical and will not listen. Misunderstandings between the sexes will tend to reinforce the social cohesion within each group. From such experiences boys will internalize the message that they need to conform with the ways other boys behave. Conformity has to be demonstrated by shared enthusiasms for things such as football and shared condemnation of other matters, such as those seen to be effeminate.

Adolescence and Identity

Adolescence is commonly seen as a time of storm and stress, in which the previously agreeable child develops into a sullen and uncooperative teenager. Although there may be a degree of exaggeration in this view there is some underlying reality. Adolescence does present a set of psychological tasks for the individual which may, for a time, seem overwhelming.

At least three factors contribute to this situation. The first is rooted in biology. The experience of puberty means that the person can now be sexually active and this fact creates a new cluster of fears and uncertainties. Adolescents may feel ill at ease with their own body and the changes to it which are beyond their control.

Second, there is the social problem that adolescents are at 'the age between'. As children they had clearly defined roles, rights and support, and as adults their position is clear. In adolescence the boundaries seem blurred, so that one teenager said to me 'Half the time they tell me that I am too young to do something and the rest of the time they tell me to grow up.'

The third task is that an adolescent has to go through what Blos (1962) called a *second individuation*. The young child has had to go through an initial individuation process in order to gain sufficient confidence and independence to leave the immediate care of the family, attend school and participate in games and play with peers. In adolescence this process has to be taken a stage further and the individual has to prepare for adulthood by making a number of self-defining choices, for example in respect to career. Another neo-Freudian, and friend of Blos, Erik Erikson (e.g. 1950 and 1968) talked about this task as that of gaining a sense of ego identity.

The word 'identity' is used widely and is often poorly defined. Part of the problem is that the term is applied to groups of people as well as individuals, so that we talk about 'corporate identity' or 'national identity'. Erikson was notoriously vague in his definitions, explaining himself by saying: 'I came to psychology from art, which may explain, if not justify, the fact that at times the reader will find me painting contexts and backgrounds where he would have me point to facts and concepts' (Erikson, 1950: 14).

I have found a reasonable working definition for personal identity to be that of a *life-script* (Head, 1997). The individual is both the author of the script, in that he or she decides what they are like and what they want to do and, at the same time, the script is used to act by. It provides a guide to behaviour.

Essentially the child is largely defined by others. His social class, place of residence and school are determined by his parents. To a considerable extent, activity is controlled by others, particularly teachers and parents. The child has only a limited scope for self-definition.

On becoming adult he has to achieve a higher degree of autonomy. He has to make choices relating to career. He has to be confident about his sexuality or sexual orientation. Finally, he has to develop some code of personal beliefs and values by which he will live. These choices need to be realistic. For example, in order to pursue a suitable career path one has to have a good sense of one's own abilities and temperament and, at the same time, a good sense of what pursuit of a particular career involves.

Marcia (e.g. 1966, 1976) suggested that identity achievement involved two processes, active thinking about the issues (Marcia used the word *crisis* for this experience, a technical term derived from psychoanalysis) and reaching a decision, what Marcia called *commitment*. Given these two processes, we can envisage four possible identity statuses to describe adolescents. Some may be slow to mature and have not yet undergone either process. Others may be fully aware of all the issues but are stuck in a moratorium, in which they cannot decide on anything. The characteristics of these young people are that they display variable moods and beliefs, swinging from idealism to cynicism, from one plan to another, in the course of a few days. This moratorium phase is not easy for the adolescent and there is consequently a psychological motivation to move on. Other adolescents will attempt to avoid the effort and possible discomfort of thinking seriously about themselves and life's options and will make decisions without thought. The psychological terminology for these people is that they have undergone foreclosure. The characteristic of foreclosed adolescents is that they tend to be inflexible and dogmatic, and unwilling to enter into reasoned discussion, because this discussion might open up the problems they have sought to avoid. Unlike the individuals experiencing moratorium, foreclosure can supply a secure resting place, at least for a while. In a sense these people have gained a fragile maturity. Finally, there will be those persons who have gained a proper sense of identity, character-ized by knowing what they want to do yet still being open to receive new ideas.

It can be seen that this process of identity achievement is so complicated that we should not be surprised that adolescence often is a time of some psychological instability and stress. Adults can help in some ways. We can provide information. Taking the obvious case of career choice we can inform them about entry requirements and likely demands of a particular type of employment. Work placements may do much more to help the youngster decide whether this is what they want to do in life. Some of the needs are less clear. Often adolescents are curious about the different ways adults live, including their lifestyles, and leisure pursuits, so not only parents and teachers, but also friends and neighbours, are scrutinized to see what role model they provide.

Alongside this need for information there is also the requirement that the adolescent actively thinks through the possibilities, yet many, from laziness or fear, may try to avoid this process. Adults can help both in the school and the home in providing a forum in which discussion of the relevant issues is encouraged. Essentially the identity script is written by the young person himself, hence attempting to impose views and values is likely to be ineffective. The discussion has be free from threat so that even the most unorthodox ideas can be debated. Only in this way can the youngster really decide what value can be attached to such views.

Despite the difficulties associated with adolescence, surveys reveal that many young people go through this phase of life without too much trauma (Murray and Dawson, 1983; Davis, 1990). Coleman (1974) suggested that the trick was for the adolescent to address one issue at a time. By focusing on the various problems in some sequence the stress could be containable and once that area had been resolved one could move on to another concern.

Nevertheless, not all adolescents have such a easy time. Erikson (1968) identified four problems which might arise. He argued that the young person had to possess a firm sense of personal identity in order to enter into a psychologically intimate relationship with another person. Being unsure about oneself meant that one did not have the confidence and trust to be open with others. Second, the adolescent may fail to develop an appropriate time perspective, necessary for planning life. As he does not think about the future he may take unreasonable risks in the present (see Bell and Bell, 1993 on adolescent risk-taking). Third, he may fail to organize his resources effectively, neglecting what is important and sometimes wasting time on what is trivial. Finally, he may adopt a negative identity, choosing dress, manner and behaviour which challenge the norms set in the home and school. Some limited experimentation with negative behaviour may be expected as part of the process of trying out various roles to see what fits oneself, but its continuation can be damaging to all involved.

So far I have outlined a generalized description of identity formation, without much regard to gender differences, but clearly some aspects may be more pertinent to young men. One factor, at least up until recent times, is that males have tended to prioritize employment in resolving their identity. They have attached significance to earning money and being able to provide for others and have gained status through being employed. Until recently many girls have placed less emphasis on their career, seeing it as subordinate to issues of marriage and motherhood.

One problem with young males is that they seem reluctant to think deeply about life's choices, preferring to undergo foreclosure. This reluctance is most marked in the realm of feelings. These are rarely discussed and some topics, such as homosexuality, are absolutely taboo. The trouble with foreclosure is that the decisions may not work out. If an adult realizes that he has made the wrong career choice, or perhaps got married despite having strong homosexual interests, then he will have a difficult task unpicking these aspects of his life. It would have been better to have made an informed and considered choice in the first instance.

A Life-Span Perspective

We have focused attention in this chapter on two periods of life, early childhood and adolescence, as these inevitably involve maturational tasks requiring changes in the self-concept. For this reason it has been common-place, particularly through the influence of psychoanalytical thinking, to see these two periods as times of storm and stress. It is beyond the scope of this book, but similar times of personal redefinition may occur in later life, notably when one ceases to be employed and when the children leave home.

Other periods of life can be traumatic, but there tends to be a qualitative difference in that the disturbance is more likely to be rooted in external events. A boy attending a primary school, right in the middle of his latency period, may be acutely unhappy, for example if he is being bullied in school or the parental marriage is breaking up. Similarly, the young adult may be stressed by the demands of coping with a young family, demands ranging from the financial to coping with sleepless nights. In some senses there is no completely carefree time; life presents one problem after another.

The significance of childhood and adolescence is that problems may be set up which impact on later life. The case of the wrong choices made in adolescence affecting adults has already been mentioned. In fact, the bulk of counselling young adults involves just these issues, reworking the identity issues of youth. Similarly, unresolved childhood problems might emerge later on. The skill and confidence to handle social relationships can be damaged if the baby failed to relate and trust those he was close to. Sometimes patterns of disturbance are created. The experience of being sexually abused may not have been totally unpleasant to a boy. He might have found some sense of excitement and importance in participating in some secret activity with an adult. Once he has undergone puberty he may wish to recapture this sense of excitement and the most obvious way for him to do this is to become an abuser.

Clearly some sense of balance has to be maintained in dealing with behavioural problems. On the one hand we must recognize that they might be symptoms of some deep-seated and unresolved earlier trauma. But, at the same time, we should avoid the common misunderstanding of psychoanalysis in failing to attribute any blame to the person here and now. Sometimes one meets the belief that someone is totally doomed to an unhappy life because they had an unhappy childhood. Some individuals use this plea to excuse themselves for their criminal behaviour. Clearly one's personal history is an influence impinging on the contemporary consciousness, but we each still possess the capacity to reflect and choose our behaviours.

4 Social Relations and the Social World

In this chapter I want to address two aspects of social life, those of personal relationships and those of social context.

Relations with Adults

In growing into adolescence some tension between the youth and his parents is almost inevitable. As we saw in the last chapter, this is a time in which the young person has to achieve the personal autonomy necessary for the development of a sense of identity. Without this sense of identity the individual is likely to be goal-less and fail to achieve adulthood satisfactorily. At some level the young recognize the need and will be pressing for ever greater independence. For a variety of reasons, parents and others responsible for the care of the young may tend to resist this pressure for greater freedom. In part, this resistance may come from the force of habit, having cared for someone for many years it is not easy to relinquish this role. But there will also be valid reasons for concern. Adults know that it can be a tough world, in which many other adults are only too willing to exploit the naiveté of youth and, in the light of such knowledge, one tends toward caution. Thus the scene is set for a time in which the adolescent is constantly claiming greater freedoms which parents and teachers are tending to resist.

Boys experience both disadvantages and advantages in this process. The disadvantage is that there is immense social pressure from peers for the individual to win this battle and demonstrate his independence. The boy who is allowed less autonomy than his peers will be labelled a wimp for failing to establish his position and will be seen to be of a low status within the group. This pressure may be so threatening that the boy pushes his case with too much vigour, leading to a series of confrontations with the parents.

The advantage boys possess is that they are seen to be at less risk than the girls and are allowed greater freedom in their movements. Boys will be allowed to be out of the home and much of their social life involves meeting their friends in the streets. Girls are more commonly kept at home and their social life is centred around the custom of them visiting each other and sitting in their bedrooms, talking and playing music. One side-effect of this gender difference is that the girl being at home is in a better position to complete her school work than her brother on the streets.

This tension between the adults and the young man can be manageable if certain processes are observed. The first is to maintain a dialogue, in which each party can make their case and the others listen. Under these circumstance some compromise might be reached. The second requirement, in order to retain control without alienation, is to adopt a stance which grants increasing freedoms to be gained at set intervals. The youngster who is given a blanket refusal to all his requests is likely to rebel. If, however, he is told that he cannot stay out to a certain hour until he reaches a particular age, then he may resent the present restriction but can be more optimistic about the future. In this fashion the boy can acquire adult freedoms over a period of a few years without having to go through a major confrontation.

Similarly, we would expect a school to treat 18-year-old students in a different fashion to those aged 11. A school which failed to make this distinction would experience difficulties in achieving its disciplinary objectives. Increasingly youngsters at the age of 16 are opting to enter college rather than continue in the same school, partly because the former is likely to allow a more adult work and social environment.

The one adult who tends to retain the intimacy with the adolescent boy for a long time is the mother. In the past she nursed and comforted him, and is aware of his fears and feelings, so he may still find that she is the one adult he can confide in. He may not want to be seen as a 'mother's boy' by his peers, so he resents going with her shopping in the neighbouring high street, but at home they retain a psychological intimacy.

Even with the mother the male wish for independence can be expressed at an early age. Arcana (1983: 9) quotes this conversation with her son aged seven:

> Daniel said today, 'When I grow up, I won't have you and my dad around anymore.' Thinking he might be worried about being left alone, I asked, 'Do you think we'll be dead by the time you are grown up?' 'No', he answered, 'I mean that I'll be free.'

Martin found that the relationship with the mother changed considerably in the teenage years. Describing those aged about 13, she wrote:

> Younger boys are still attached to their mothers as 'mom', as a care-taker who fulfils their needs. ... These younger boys talked about how their mothers affected them and how they affected their mothers.
>
> (1996: 96)

But she said of those aged about 17:

> Older boys, however, disidentify with their mothers. ... As teenage boys
> grow older, there is more and more pressure to be masculine. One's
> attachment to his mother psychologically and practically gets in the way
> of masculinity.

(1996: 97)

With the father, assuming that there is a father at home, the position tends
to be slightly different. In public being with the father is less demeaning as
they may share such masculine interests as football, fishing and cars.
Although the boy may begin to prefer the company of peers, the shared
interests he has with his father are also the interests of his peers, and as such
are socially acceptable. Within the home the relationship with the father
may be more fraught than with the mother. The father may see it as his
responsibility to assert control and the male style of discourse is more direct
and confrontational. Relationships with the father can therefore be very
volatile, combining a mix of the comradeship of shared interests with the
conflicts over rights and responsibilities.

There can also be an element of competition within the relationship. For
the first time the father may find that his son can defeat him on the sports
field and one middle-aged man told me of his sadness when walking down
the street with his son to notice that the young ladies they passed looked at
the son rather than at him. This recognition that your son is now stronger
and more attractive than oneself requires some shift both in self-image and
in the family relationships.

One thing which can bring father and son together is the shared concern
with paid work, particularly if the son enters the same business as his father,
and a concomitant reluctance to take the primary responsibility for much of
the work in the home. Edley and Wetherell (1995: 117) quote evidence that
only about 1 per cent of men take the main or sole responsibility for
housework or child care, but 83 per cent assume such responsibility for
household repairs. They comment, 'These differences indicate the presence
of a sexual division of labour within the home which is as pervasive and
important for defining masculinity and men's experiences as class divisions
in paid work' (1995: 115).

What is often lacking in the father and son relationship is the capacity to
talk about intimate feelings. It might be presumed that this is the arena in
which the youth can learn about sexual behaviour, but the evidence is that
although girls talk freely with their mothers, boys tend to learn more from
their peers than their fathers. The starting point for this non-communication
is likely to be the reluctance of many men to talk to anyone about their
feelings, and this taboo is apparent to the youth, who then by a process of
social reproduction learns that masculinity involves such reticence. We

might modify Chodorow's book title to describe this process as the reproduction of fathering.

A further factor in the contemporary world is the concern about child abuse so that many fathers are reluctant to touch or talk about sexual matters with their children. Moore and Rosenthal refer to 'the incest taboo', suggesting that it inhibits discussion:

> Discussions about sex are a form of social interaction and, in the family context, these discussions are often embarrassing, even when both parents and adolescents have liberal attitudes and are comfortable about talking with peers about sexual matters.
>
> (1993: 65)

Fathers may compensate for their inability to talk about feelings with their sons by adopting a hearty, playful relationship. As Miedzian reports:

> Research reveals that fathers, especially, tend to become deeply disturbed by any behavior in their sons that is not typically masculine. ... parents, especially fathers, who want to make sure that their sons grow up strong and tough often overstimulate them from an early age. They toss them about more, act loud and tough rather than soft and gentle.
>
> (1992: 83)

Thus the social reproduction of masculine qualities is enhanced through this interaction.

Although tensions commonly exist between youth and adults they do not represent the whole story. In fact, there is a continuing dynamic between the wish for independence and, at the same time, for interest and support. Montemayor et al. sum up the situation, arguing the existence of 'two clusters of relational constructs: those emphasizing relative distance during adolescence – conflict, individuation, psychological separation and autonomy: and those emphasizing interpersonal connectedness – trust, intimacy, closeness, relative positive affect, and communication' (1994: 2).

Young people need adults for a variety of reasons. They want people to take interest in them. While teaching in a boarding school I found that boys as old as 17 or 18 felt rejected by being sent away to school. One such boy complained to me that his parents showed no interest in him so that although he was the best athlete in the school his parents never came to see him perform.

One process which aids identity formation is for the youngster to compare himself with adults, noting where they are alike or different. By recognizing similar interests, values or characteristics they can see a possible role for themselves. They also need information about possible careers and lifestyles, and communication with adults can provide it. Finally, it is not sufficient for this information to be passively absorbed. The youth has to 'own it', by actively considering the possibilities, and some form of a dialogue with an adult should help stimulate such thought.

Social Stratification and the Sibling Society

Although we have established the ongoing importance for young men of them maintaining a close relationship and significant dialogue with adults there is evidence that currently such communication is becoming rarer. I will use the two overlapping concepts contained in the sub-title of this section to describe the situation.

We usually think of social divisions as being principally vertical, so, for example, that most members of the same family will be within the same social class. What has become increasingly common is a form of horizontal stratification, in which the young spend nearly all their time with peers. In part, this effect has come from the widespread collapse of family life. The extended family is rarer. Many nuclear families are headed by a single parent. At the same time many alternative venues in which adults and adolescent boys meet, such as the Boy Scouts, Boys Brigade and Youth Clubs, have in many areas almost disappeared. Currently I am supervizing the research of someone looking at boys' friendships in the East End of London. Thirty years ago, when Willmott (1969) made his famous study in the same area of London, there was abundance of such venues. Now there is practically nothing. There is not even a cinema in the district. As a consequence there is little opportunity for the youth to meet adults who might add to and complement what the parents can do.

It is not that the young men are universally hostile to adults. This same researcher has started an informal football club with a number of young men in their late teens. They play in a local park on Sunday mornings and the enterprise has flourished as more and more have asked if they can join. The boys had been bored and welcomed the chance to participate in an organized activity. They clearly did not resent the presence of the two adults who manage the initiative.

I have borrowed the second concept, that of the sibling society, from a book by Bly (1996). I have reservations about some of Bly's work, which will become apparent later in this book, but believe that he has touched on something important here.

He takes the argument about horizontal stratification further. The starting point is the same as mine, that the young spend an increasing amount of their time with their peers and less with adults. Bly in essence argues that they then fail to grow up and enter adulthood still in a group who have the ideas and norms of adolescence. He goes on to suggest that corresponding to the biological life-span, from childhood to old age, there should be social and psychological development. Furthermore, it is through people of different ages interacting that the young can be initiated into their culture and values of society and, at the same time, the adults can gain a sense of achievement in acting as mentors. He argues that we now live in a 'flat society' in which social and psychological maturation is ignored or undervalued and where adults too often behave like a crowd of envious and competitive siblings.

I cannot do justice in this book to his broad treatment of this topic, but believe that he is right in drawing attention to the loss of opportunities to relate and learn from older people, with the corresponding increase in the influence of the peer group.

Boys Together

We have already noted that quite young children spontaneously tend to play in single-sex groups and this habit marks the beginning of the single-sex peer group which will dominate much of the life of boys and young men.

Part of the group cohesion simply comes from shared interests, but the social dynamics are such that the pressures to conform to the group are much greater than can be accounted for by this factor. We must go back to the description of how young boys are reared and note that they tend to be weak in relational skills but develop a strong sense of independence. Each boy joining a group starts with his own agenda and a lack of empathy with others. Initially, this individual selfishness leads to conflicts, blows and tears. After a while, as they mature, boys develop strategies for managing this potential for aggression, by creating hierarchies and rules of conduct.

The existence of a hierarchy or hegemony in which the dominant boy, being either older or stronger than the others, can make the final decision, allows the group to function effectively. Without such a leader it disintegrates into an anarchy of competing voices. Consequently, much of the initial activity of a new group is concerned with establishing the hierarchy. In addition to the leader, other roles are available, including that of seeking the protection of the leader. Sometimes a relatively small boy can gain a significant status by possessing an advanced sense of humour and is then tolerated as the court jester.

Within informal friendship groups the structure is not static and the dominant boys are ever likely to face criticism and challenge which creates tension. Within formal work groups the hierarchy is stabilized by creating recognizable ranks, such as the multitude of layers within army or police forces. In business there is likely to be a carefully graduated range of office cars provided according to seniority.

These qualities of competition and hierarchy seem to be totally pervasive. Boys constantly bicker, interrupting and challenging each other. They will act out mock fights and welcome situations, whether playing football or a video game, in which they can give expression to the rivalry. Even in the early school years the habit and culture of mock fights is evident (Jordan, 1995), and the sense of competition extends into adulthood, with anxieties about having a big enough house, an expensive car, winning at games ranging from golf and squash to darts, and even competing to grow the largest onions or marrows in a local show.

This competitive spirit can be used to motivate boys in dealing with school work, but it is a double-edged sword. One problem is that competition must produce losers, as well as winners, and hence can damage the motivation of some. Additionally, there is evidence that boys can be concerned solely with competing with each other, by working quickly, so that they fail to consider whether they really understand what they are doing.

Membership of the boys' group demands acceptance of certain rules. Some can be explicit, such as the conforming to dress codes. The concept of fair play, of sharing things equally among the group, is commonly crucial. In fact, this sense of sharing allows boys to work happily alongside each other even if they are not actively co-operating. Askew and Ross (1988) describe what tends to happen if single-sex pairs of pupils are asked to paint a picture together. Girls will negotiate in order to identify something to which both can contribute. Boys may draw a line down the centre of the paper and each then work independently on his half.

Some of the rules are implicit, specifically in not doing certain things, such as talking about fears and feelings, or behaving in any way which is seen to be effete or effeminate. It is probably the fear of transgressing these taboos which brings about the observed poverty of discourse within groups of boys. Rather than risk saying something which is unacceptable the boys narrow the range of subjects to things which are clearly safe, such as sport. Jokes are valued, but expressions of doubt are not. Somewhere like the changing room of a rugby club demonstrates these constraints most clearly. In some respects there is great intimacy with communal showers, shared jokes and the singing of rugby songs. At the same time there are great constraints so that personal anxieties are not aired. Physical contact is similarly structured, so that hearty horse-play is common, but anything suggesting tenderness or affection would be absolutely unacceptable. Boys soon learn the rules of the group, conform and then impose them on others.

These male groups not only prescribe what is perceived to be soft or effeminate but reward the macho qualities of being cool, hard and risk-taking. Individuals may feel forced to demonstrate their masculine credentials by engaging in some risky activity such as driving a car at dangerously high speeds, fighting members of rival groups or gangs, or being willing to drink more lager than anyone else. One of the difficulties in Personal and Social Education programmes with boys is that see it as unmanly to avoid risk. In their view a real man will not use a condom to avoid the risk of HIV/AIDS or decline the use of drugs.

A group gains its sense of identity not only by inclusion, of those with similar interests and loyalties, but also by exclusion. Coleman (1974) reported that the commonest worry among boys aged between 13 and 15 is that of rejection by the peer group. The rejected individual has few friends, is seen to be of low status and is vulnerable to bullying as there is no certainty that others will protect him.

The same-sex peer group can provide valuable support at a time when the young man is attempting to reduce his dependence on his family and before he is ready to enter into adult relationships. Against this positive side must be set the fact that the group can develop into a gang. Bullying, vandalism, football crowd hooliganism and much youth crime is a group activity. Individually, the boys would rarely venture into these acts.

These limitations of the male groups would not matter that much if they were balanced by the boys having access to alternative social groups, particularly with adults. It is in this context that the problems of horizontal social stratification, mentioned earlier in this chapter, become apparent. The work of Maguire (1997) illustrates this point. In looking at the career plans of teenagers she found that the girls had talked to a wide range of people, adults and peers, and were consequently well informed about possibilities and choices. The boys tended to talk exclusively to their peers and discussion of career plans did not form much of their discourse. Consequently the boys were frequently muddled. One academically able boy spoke about an ambition to become a doctor of medicine alongside the statement that he did not really want to continue in full-time education, but would prefer to seek some form of apprenticeship. Clearly he had no idea that a medical career would require the gaining of good A level grades followed by five or six years in higher education.

Gendered Discourses

The differences in the dynamics of single-sex groups presents one of the difficulties of boys and girls in communicating and understanding each other. Talk among boys is marked by competition, so that each speaker is more inclined to assert his own beliefs rather than listen and respond to others. In contrast, the discourse among girls prioritizes relational aspects more, so that each speaker tends to refer to others before making their own point. Within mixed groups the girls find it difficult to cope with the competitive bickering of the boys and complain that the boys do not listen to them. The boys are made uneasy by the fact that girls ignore the implicit taboos by asking about feelings and fears.

These differences are more of social habit than genetic and can be overcome. The starting point within a coeducational school is to ensure that work takes place within mixed groups, otherwise interaction is bound to be limited. Various tactics can be undertaken to ensure that the students listen to each other, for example by having an exercise in which each person has to report what others say in a discussion, rather than giving their own view. Initially boys often find this task difficult, as their mind-set is more towards coming up with a good answer than in listening to others. There is greater educational significance to this point than may be obvious. Part of the academic underachievement of boys is that they tend to work too hastily and carelessly. They do not read the question carefully. By working with girls they may be forced to slow down, listen, and gain a better appreciation of the task before attempting to address it.

The gender difference in discourse has been widely discussed, including in such popular books as *You Just Don't Understand: Women and Men in Conversation* (Tannen, 1991) and *Men Are from Mars, Women Are from Venus* (Gray, 1992). Part of the interest in these works arises from the experiences of counsellors dealing with problems of personal relationships. Men and women may find that their different histories of personal interactions gets in the way of communicating. A woman may be concerned about the reluctance of her partner to reveal his feelings and will feel compelled to press him on these issues. Meanwhile he is becoming increasingly embarrassed by the discussion, as she is not observing the restraints he learnt with male groups, and becomes ever more terse and reticent. In this fashion the dynamic between the pair can lead to an ever increasing division.

Perhaps more relevant to our concerns is the work of Gilligan (1982). She found that male and female college students tended to employ different ways of thinking and talking about events. The men tended to adopt an analytical, logical, rule-seeking approach. They would take a legalistic stance based on clear rules, such as driving at 30 miles per hour is legal but at 31 is not. Women tended to look less at the precise details but would take a more holistic view, seeking to locate issues within context. Thus in conversation men and women may have somewhat different agendas. It must be stressed that neither alternative is overall better or more correct than the other, but with a specific task one may be better. If, for example, someone is driving a car and it suddenly breaks down, then it is reasonable to assume only one thing is malfunctioning. It would be an odd coincidence if several parts malfunctioned at the same time. The task, therefore, is to locate that one bit and ignore everything else about the car. In other situations an alternative approach would be better. For example, in dealing with environmental issues it is necessary to consider the total context affected by some action, such as removing a wood or building a road, as the variables interact with each other. Removing a wood might affect drainage in the area, it will alter light penetration and wind effects, and change both the local flora and animal life.

Although effective communication between men and women may not always be easy, it can be the vital element in maintaining personal relationships, but also can give rise to a broader understanding of issues and problems within a wider context. The two modes of thinking and talking complement each other, and a richer understanding of our society is gained by making some form of synthesis.

Early Heterosexual Experience

The words which are commonly associated with heterosexuality include 'commonplace', 'normal' or 'natural', and these terms might be taken to imply that the process of young men entering into such relationships is non-problematic. In fact, there are a variety of obstacles, in addition to differences in styles of discourse.

One obvious factor is that of different maturation rates. Girls reach puberty about eighteen months to two years before boys, so they have gone through much of the physical and mental changes while the boys are still puny and childlike. At this stage girls tend to be more interested in older boys rather than boys of their peer group. In addition, the actual experience of puberty is different for the two sexes. For boys, other than the relatively minor matters of acne and having to shave, it rarely presents any problems (Gaddis and Brooks-Gunn, 1985). Girls face two difficulties. Prendergast (1992) made a survey of about 500 girls and found that over 80 per cent complained of experiencing period pain on occasions, and 65 per cent experienced it most or all months. Other common symptoms included headaches, feeling unwell and depression. The second concern of girls is that they may become pregnant, which is not made easier by the fact that many boys have a cavalier attitude to this possibility. Puberty, therefore, is seen by boys to be a pleasurable occurrence, marking the higher status of maturation and allowing one to experience the joys of sex, but for girls it is understandably seen with greater ambivalence.

Boys and girls, therefore, approach each other after puberty with different agendas. For the boy, physical sexual experience is pleasurable and therefore he seeks it. Meanwhile the girl is likely to be more tentative. The peer pressure differs, too. Girls who are believed to be sexually available are likely to be labelled 'slags' (Lees, 1986) while for the boys the position is reversed and they need to establish their heterosexual credentials. Not to enter into heterosexual activity causes the boy to be seen to be a wimp or gay by his male peers, so he is forced to proceed, although he may not really be ready to do so. Holland et al., in their study of early male sexual experience, quote one young man as saying: 'Men see it as something that has got to be done, that is what I think, so your friends don't tease you' (1993: 14). The increased permissiveness with respect to much of sexual behaviour means that young people gain experience earlier in life. In the most detailed survey of sexual behaviour in Britain, Wellings et al. (1994) found that 27.6 per cent of males born in the first half of the 1970s had sexual intercourse prior to the age of 16, the legal limit. For those born in the early 1940s the corresponding figure was 13.9 per cent and for the early 1930s it was 5.8 per cent. Although the greater openness about sex has many benefits it does at the same time increase pressure on the young to become involved.

Part of the problem for young men is that they believe that they have to take the initiative and find this difficult when they themselves are inexperienced. In an egalitarian society we might argue for men and women to be equally able to initiate sexual activity, but in one sense this is not possible. The timing, duration and frequency of intercourse is dependent on the male being aroused. Young men are conscious of this fact and enter into early relationships with anxiety about their ability to perform. It is true that male youth often approach sexual activity from a selfish perspective, interested in themselves but indifferent to their partner, but this behaviour is more understandable once we appreciate the pressures they face. Holland et al. (1998) demonstrate that this male dominance of heterosexual activity continues for some time. Fortunately, as they mature and gain confidence, most men begin to relate more fully with their partner.

In many respects the response of young men to heterosexuality typifies much of their behaviour. Outwardly they appear confident and successful but this may mask many anxieties. They have to appear knowledgeable and mature to their contemporaries, so that they scorn formal sex education, claiming that they already know all about it, when in reality their arrogance hides ignorance. Hill (1995) quotes young men in Further Education dismissing the idea of using condoms to prevent the spread of HIV/AIDS on the grounds that they always withdrew before reaching their climax.

Homophobia and Homosexuality

For the majority of boys the experience of homosexuality is absent or minimal, but for all that, the influence of a homophobic culture is pervasive and powerful. The roots are deep, going back to early Christian and Jewish teaching, but the prejudice remains strong. In the various attempts to liberalize the legal situation for males, ranging from 1967 to 1998, much of the opposition has been framed in emotive language and makes bizarre appeals to the notion that the Classical Greek and Roman civilizations collapsed because of this sexual activity. Liberalization, it has been argued, would destroy the social and economic strength of the country, a claim which ignores the evidence that the most prosperous parts of Europe, Scandinavia, Holland, Germany and France, have long adopted a more liberal regime.

The legal constraints have been enforced with surprising zeal over the years, with police using such questionable tactics as *agents provocateurs*, despite Home Office instructions not to do so. Men have been convicted on the basis of uncorroborated evidence from their partners, who would have been equally guilty but were granted immunity to give evidence. There have been a number of instances in recent years when men in their early twenties, who have robbed and killed an older man, have been able to reduce a murder charge to one of manslaughter, by claiming that the older man made a pass at them. A young woman would unlikely to be able to use such a story in her defence, even though she is less able to physically defend herself.

This constant expression of homophobic attitudes is quickly recognized by the young and is absorbed into the group culture. Alongside hegemony, the main characteristic of male groups is compulsive heterosexuality. Research with male adolescents reveals that any discussion of homosexuality is taboo, so that the interview will be jeopardized by mentioning the topic. Boys seem willing in class discussions to admit that discrimination and bullying of those of a different race is wrong, but plead that homosexual men deserve attack. The extent of their prejudice is captured by Nayak and Kehily (1996). One boy in a school has been shown a film about HIV/AIDS, which included an interview with a gay man. He told a friend, who then asked 'And you sat and watched it?' In defence, the original boy replied, 'We had to! We had to sit and watch it, we had no choice, we had to stay and watch it' (1996: 222). Clearly he felt that he was either being labelled as gay, in being interested in the film, or being a wimp, in quietly sitting down and watching the film.

This homophobic ethic is unfortunate for all. For those in the minority, who think that they might be gay, have the additional problem of being unable to talk matters over with their friends. They have to camouflage their feelings and worries. Given that many parents are also unsympathetic, often to the extent of turning the young man out of his home, it not surprising that many gay youth are desperately and unnecessarily unhappy. The evidence is that a mother will eventually accept her son's sexuality, as her primary concern is for his well-being, whatever that may involve, but fathers appear to find their own masculinity being threatened in producing a son who may be seen as not being wholly male.

For the majority, homophobia provides an excuse for harassment and bullying. Those deemed to be 'poofs' are legitimate targets. Furthermore, the boys will claim that their intolerant attitude receives tacit support from many teachers in the school. It is certainly notable that over 90 per cent of the schools that have policy statements about bullying, and refer to gender and race, omit reference to sexual orientation.

Although in many respects there has been a change in recent decades, with more open discussion of homosexuality and the growth of the gay economy, there has developed the paradox that greater awareness has sometimes led to greater constraint. Hickson (1996) surveyed the sexual experiences of men who had been to public schools and found considerable evidence both of the former prevalence of homosexual activity among the boys and of a laissez-faire attitude among the staff. It was argued that if teenage boys were kept in a boarding school then such activity was inevitable. It was also recognized that such experience would not change the ultimate sense of sexual identity of the young man, but would simply serve to confirm or deny his orientation. Writing about the attitudes of the authorities of Oxford University in the 1920s, Carpenter (1989) suggested that they were more worried about male undergraduates entering into heterosexual relationships with women in the town than with homosexual relationships among themselves. Issues of social class and money were seen to be crucial, as the heterosexual relationship might lead to pregnancy, causing the undergraduate either to marry someone of a different class or spend money to settle with her and her family.

With a greater awareness of homosexuality has arisen greater concern. Interestingly, it was in 1967, the year in which Parliament relaxed the law on homosexual behaviour, that the first traditional public school, Marlborough College, admitted girls. Hickson (1996) argued that one of the main motives for this change, which was followed by many other similar schools, was to reduce the risk of homosexual activity in the schools. Hickson also found a parallel change in attitude among the boys, so that the most popular and respected boys now have to possess such traditional qualities of being good at sports but, in addition, have an attractive girlfriend. Institutions have also grown increasingly nervous about the possibility of staff making sexual contact with boys, so that the leading schools have gone beyond the legal requirements, such as using the register of sex offenders, in setting up their own vetting procedures and information exchange on applicants. Reference has been made earlier in this chapter to the decline in youth clubs and scout groups. Part of the trouble seems to be that adults who do voluntary work with youth are now suspected of having a sexual motive and potential helpers are reluctant to expose themselves to such a slur.

Just as the greater permissiveness has had a paradoxical effect in relation to heterosexual behaviour, by both making issues more open but also creating some increased pressures, so the greater general tolerance of homosexuality in the wider society has increased awareness and enhanced homophobia among youth.

The Social Context

In the opening chapter of this book it was pointed out that inevitably there will be many generalizations about young men which are open to some caveats. Various social factors, including social class and ethnicity, interact with gender, so that certain sub-groups of youth will have different experiences to those of the majority. Probably the best tactic for coping with this issue is to note the exceptions and differences as each aspect of male behaviour is discussed, but it seems appropriate to insert at this point in the text a reminder of the importance of these social variables.

One of the simplest examples is that of geography as a controlling influence on employment prospects. For many years the area running to the west and south-west of London has prospered with new industries. The M4 corridor has been described as the Silicon Valley of Britain. Unemployment in towns such as Basingstoke and Swindon has generally been at about 2 per cent of the labour force. Such a figure indicates no significant unemployment as the social mobility of people changing jobs or moving into the area always places some people on the unemployed list. In some of the old industrial heartlands of the north of England unemployment rates have commonly been ten or twenty times greater and hence the prospects for boys in school will seem to be very different.

Social class has long been a focus of attention within sociology. If again we choose to look at employment we find Willis (1977) describing the traditional unskilled working-class youth. Rooted in their thinking is a sense of community with their peers of similar background and opposition to those perceived to be from a different class. These values lead to school being valued principally as a social institution in which friendships with peers are strengthened, and teachers being seen as people to be resisted. Consequently, learning of the formal school curriculum tends to be limited. On moving into industrial employment the camaraderie with work mates and resistance to the employers continue the pattern. As Willis points out, the boys behave in such a way that they lock themselves into unskilled labour, hence the sub-title he gave to his book: *How Working Class Kids Get Working Class Jobs.* Since Willis wrote this book the situation has deteriorated for these young men as so many jobs for unskilled workers have been lost. By contrast middle-class youth have been more entrepreneurial, pursuing the areas of the labour market where well-paid employment exists. In the past twenty years we have seen the entry of these young men into banking, computing and allied areas. The underlying cause seems to be that middle-class students are encouraged by parents and friends to be more individualistic and competitive, to set high aims for themselves, and not to pay too much attention to tradition.

With respect to ethnicity the picture is complex. We know that pupils from most Asian groups do very well at school, while Afro-Caribbean pupils fare the least well. The problem is to identify with certainty the causal pattern. Family background provides part of the explanation, with Asian families being close-knit and Asian parents maintaining tight control. Even here the situation is complex as there are big differences in the ways boys and girls are treated. One of the commonest complaints I receive from students is from Asian girls saying how difficult it is for them to cope living within two conflicting cultures. At school or college they mix freely with young men, but at home they may be allowed little contact with males outside their family.

Afro-Caribbean boys present the most worrying figures, with high truancy, crime and unemployment rates. In some parts of south London 60 per cent of black youth cannot find employment on leaving school. A variety of explanations have been given, with the high incidence of single-parent families being quoted as one factor.

We must not make the mistake of assuming that we are dealing with a homogeneous group. In a study of a London school, Sewell (1998), identified four sub-groups among the Afro-Caribbean youth. The largest element, making up 41 per cent of the total, make friends across ethnic boundaries and are not in conflict with the school. They do, however, find it difficult both to conform to the norms of the school and maintain good relations with all their Afro-Caribbean peers. The second group, 31 per cent of the total, are in a state of conflict. On one hand they accept the aims of schooling, largely through parental influence, but reject the means, the actuality of their experience of school. The third group, about 6 per cent of the total, are labelled by Sewell as retreatist. They do not enter into the ethos or activity of the school but they make no overt resistance. They spend the day aimlessly hanging around the corridors, trying to avoid attracting attention. Finally, there are the overt rebels, who largely socialize with other Afro-Caribbean youth and resist schooling.

There have been various claims and counter-claims as to whether the problem lies in the Afro-Caribbean culture or with racial conflict in this country. Parry (1997) describes the situation in Jamaica, where there is widespread concern about the marginalization of young males. The boys seem to have a very rigid, macho sense of masculinity, which expresses itself in a contempt for teachers, who are largely female in that country. To what extent these attitudes have been imported into Britain is debatable, not least because a very different ethic exists on some of the other Caribbean islands.

While writing this book a group of Afro-Caribbean youth, aged about 17, came up from Brixton to talk to me about their position. They clearly feared that the prospects for them were grim and sought help in knowing how to address the issue. Many of these young men believe that they are labelled as making unsatisfactory workers by virtue of their race, so they never get offered a job. If the boys have such poor experience and expectations then it is not surprising that they cannot see the point in pursuing their academic studies very seriously. Maybe the concern shown by these youngsters is a harbinger of better things to come. I was impressed by their initiative in seeking help and advice, but, at the same time, was worried whether I, as a middle-class white man, was in the best position to help. What emerged most strongly from the discussion was their failure to identify mentors among the adult men within their own community. As with so many of the issues raised in this chapter, the relationship between adults and the young seems to be crucial.

5 The Male Psyche

Despite the cautionary note at the end of the last chapter, reminding us of the considerable diversity which can exist among young men, there remains clear evidence of common qualities in their psychological dispositions. Sometimes the social, biological and personal factors are in opposition, and the resolution reached by an individual will depend on their relative strengths. Often these contributory influences will reinforce each other. For example, it is commonly observed that males tend to be the aggressive sex. Reference can be made to animal behaviour to postulate a biological cause. But any such biological effect is reinforced by social forces in which boys are told to stand up for themselves and compete with their peers. Young men often gain the impression that parents and teachers would prefer them to enter into a fight rather than be seen to be a wimp. Certainly the traditional public schools have emphasized the importance of such contact sports as rugby and the value of the cadet corps. One of the most bizarre manifestations of this desire to be macho I have met was when I taught in an American high school. I found that some of the boys deliberately broke the bones in their hand, in the belief that in healing the bone would become larger, making the hand heavier and stronger for karate. I do not know whether this belief is valid, but in any event, but such extreme behaviour involving self-injury must surely be undesirable.

We must also appreciate that the qualities associated with men are not necessarily undesirable. In writing a book about academic underachievement and behavioural problems I may give too negative an image of male youth. Aggression may be seen among lager louts fighting each other at the end of a drunken evening. It is also the quality which allows young men to fight for their country in times of war. Looking at the trench conditions and fighting in the 1914–18 war, for example, the wonder is that so many men endured the appalling conditions and high mortality rates. A combination of idealism, the patriotic wish to fight for their country, fear of being labelled a coward and the ability to acquire a degree of detachment about their situation combined to yield extraordinary heroism. Not only did these men have to face the risk of injury or death themselves but they had to inflict injury and death on others, on an on-going basis, day after day.

Similarly, the characteristic of young men to take risks can lead to appalling car accidents, fights and injury pursuing dangerous sports. It is also the characteristic which helps these men achieve success professional and academic life. They go beyond a high level of competence in an effort to stand out, being markedly dynamic, creative or original, and if they succeed in this ambition the risk-taking is abundantly awarded.

Until recently it might have seemed odd to write about the psychology of men, for historically nearly all mainstream psychology had been developed by men, and frequently they based their generalizations about human behaviour solely on the study of males. For example, it took Gilligan (1982) to point out that Kohlberg's model of moral development was based on a study of young men and was not appropriate for women. Freud notoriously despaired of understanding the psychology of women. So a male-centred model predominated with occasional references to females as being inconveniently somewhat different. The rise of feminist-inspired studies from the 1960s onwards has had two effects. It has placed women in the centre as the subjects for study. More pertinently to us in the context of this book, it has asked different questions, and has opened up issues which the men had tended to neglect. It then became apparent that the previous psychology had a deficient description of male development. Questions about why men made up such a high proportion of criminals and the homeless had not been fully explored. Specifically it drew attention to the affective aspects of men, feelings and fears, the very topics men usually try to avoid.

In essence much of this chapter represents a summary and synthesis of points which have been discussed previously. For this reason I have not gone into detail, or given many references to the associated literature.

A Sense of Struggle

One common issue to emerge in discussion with boys is their sense that they have to strive for success. Nothing comes to them naturally by a process of maturation. They have to compete and, even if successful, they only retain their high status by demonstrating time and time again their ability to win. Men have tended to be both the winners in our society, gaining the glittering prizes, and also the losers, the homeless and the criminal. They are the bullies and the bullied.

One is reminded of the story given by Frazer in *The Golden Bough* (1922), in which the High Priest enjoys success having gained his position by assassinating his predecessor. However, at the same time, he walks in fear, knowing that other, younger men are waiting for him, knife in hand, ready to assassinate him in turn. This sense of never being at rest and always having to prove oneself seems ubiquitous. For example, Cohen writes: 'When I was a little boy I was told to be a man. When my marriage was breaking up my mother told me "to be a man". By this, she seemed to mean that I shouldn't go back to my wife' (1990: 1).

An analogy can be made with the early history of the boy. As a foetus he has to undergo the effects of testosterone switching his development off the natural female path on to that of becoming a male. As a young child he has to dis-identify with his mother and learn to become a man. Frequently boys make comments such as 'No one tells you how to become a man.' They see it as their challenging task to unlock the secret themselves. They recognize that masculinity is largely defined in the negative, in not being certain things, such as being soft, effete, feminine or gay, but they express uncertainty about what they actually should be.

Kilmartin summed up the situation:

> boys do not get nearly as much of an opportunity to observe their fathers and other adult males. Therefore, they must extrapolate a good deal in constructing a sense of what masculinity is. Boys must fill in large gaps in the information. ... There is also the tendency to be masculine by avoiding feminine behaviors. When males do so in rigid and extreme ways, they cut themselves off from a large collection of potentially adaptive and satisfying experiences.
>
> (1994: 89)

How can the positive qualities of maleness be developed? Obviously fathers and other male mentors can help, but the relationship between father and son is often marked more by a gentle rivalry than by a willingness to talk openly about feelings and fears. Boys are also made aware of the punitive attitudes of peers to what they regard as unacceptable in behaviour or attitude, so the individual is always on the defensive, monitoring what he says and does in order to avoid giving others any ammunition with which to attack him. As we have already noted, boys will undergo considerable hardship at sports in order to gain reaffirmation of their masculine credentials.

Difficulties in Handling Emotions

The situation is best up by Seidler when he wrote:

> I would argue that the sharp demarcation in our moral culture, which was given its clearest secular expression in Kant's ethical theory, between rationality which is conceived as mental and as a source of our freedom, and our emotions and desires which are treated as externally influencing and determining our behaviour, has shaped our conceptions of masculinity. ... The very universality of our reason has somehow worked to impersonalize our experience. It has made us strangers to our emotional lives.
>
> (1989: 50–2)

As with any other quality, the expression and control of emotions develops through practice, yet boys are denied the opportunities to make such expression. One of the comments often made to me by teachers is that the boys seem to lack the vocabulary to articulate their feelings. Only a very limited range of emotions can be shown. Anger is far more permissible than affection or fear. In fact, fierce anger can give status among peers as indicating that one is hard and not willing to be pushed around. One can show grief at the loss of a pet animal, or in losing at football, but not about other people. A boy cannot afford to show feelings which would be judged as inappropriate by his peers. Reticence is the safe defence. In this fashion the youth experience great emotional poverty.

Consequently, within marriages it is commonplace for the wife to have to assume the role of handling the various tensions which can arise between the partners and with their children. The husband lacks the resources and skills to deal with such matters. At its extreme this suppression of emotion becomes dangerous and the censorship mechanism becomes incapable of holding feelings dammed up for any longer. Emotional outbursts can then occur, so that what starts as love may end up as abuse, and what starts as anger becomes murderous.

Men are at some level aware of the dangers and one powerful concern is to maintain control, over themselves and over others with whom they deal. Through control, their own feelings can be managed or canalized. By controlling others, or the situation in which they are, they avoid having to address things which cause unease or are beyond their competence. Without a sense of control they cannot cope. One young man I was counselling threatened to castrate himself as his sexual interests and fantasies contradicted his strong moral beliefs. If he could not control his sexual feelings by will-power he believed that he would have to reassert control by surgery.

Recently there has been a genre of literature emerging which highlights the dangers contained in separating the affective from the cognitive, usually to the detriment of the former. Damasio's (1994) title *Descartes' Error* locates this separation in the seventeenth-century enlightenment. Goleman's (1996) book, *Emotional Intelligence*, is summed up on its cover:

> Daniel Goleman argues that our view of human intelligence is too narrow, and our emotions play a greater role in thought, decision making and individual success than is commonly acknowledged. Emotional intelligence includes self-awareness and impulse control, persistence, zeal and motivation, empathy and social deftnesss.

We have there a good starting point for an agenda of work with young men.

The Need for Rules and Categories

Reference has already been made to Gilligan's (1982) study of the ways in which males and females address issues. The former are more apt to follow a logical approach, seeking to establish patterns of cause and effect, and the rules of procedure. Women tend to be less rule-bound and adopt a more wide-ranging approach. Men will try to judge matters in a neutral, legalistic fashion while women are more apt to display empathy and allow their feelings to transcend legalistic concerns.

The main concern to be noted in this chapter is that men seem to need rules. They work better in an environment in which they clearly understand what is required from them and how they are expected to behave. This finding has implications for schools and the ways they are organized and discipline is maintained.

Alongside the belief in rules comes that of dividing things into categories. Distinctions are drawn, for example between home and work, men and women, and overlap or ambiguity produces unease. Perhaps it is their practical experience that makes women less aware of the home/work divide, but they seem also to be less bound by concepts such as gender rules. The extreme case of the male thinking is to treat those of other categories as the Other (see Paechter, 1998). In this event discrimination or inequity can be justified. It must be remembered that much of the cruelty practised in the Nazi concentration camps was carried out by doctors of medicine, who could morally justify their actions by the belief that they were carrying out their experiments on another category of beings, Jews, Gypsies and homosexuals, who were sub-human. Without being able to create such categories it would be difficult to justify their actions to themselves.

Given the characteristics of disliking or distrusting emotions and seeking a world organized by rules and categories, we can see the appeal of science to the male mind. It provides an arena where the male strengths of logical analysis can be beneficial and in which the threats presented by emotional concerns can be avoided. In a nutshell, they are happier in dealing with objects and things, rather than people.

The Risk of Foreclosure

We have seen that an essential task of adolescence and early adulthood is to acquire a sense of personal identity, that is developing a realistic plan or script for dealing with adulthood. The two requirements for gaining a mature sense of identity are to consider with care the issues and possibilities and then reach a firm decision. Without a decision the youth is locked into an extended adolescence in which there are no real goals, and hence no real effort to attain goals.

Perhaps the other incomplete position, that of foreclosure, presents the greater difficulties. In this case the individual avoids the effort, and possibly discomfort, of thinking deeply about himself and what he is going to do in life. He simply makes sudden decisions or commitments, without thought. He will accept uncritically ideas from others. Foreclosure is common among young men, as their social discourse, and to a considerable extent their private thinking, does not allow various possibilities to be debated. Because it would be absolutely unacceptable to consider for a moment that they might be homosexual they will firmly foreclose into heterosexuality. Similarly they will not consider careers which might be judged as effeminate. The danger is that, through lack of thought, they may make choices which do not work out for them. At some stage in later life they will begin to appreciate that their strengths, abilities, beliefs or sexual interests are other than those allowed for in their plans. This realization is very threatening. They have lost their sense of certainty and have to undergo the painful task of thinking issues through again and perhaps starting their life on a different basis.

Had these people been more able to undergo this process in adolescence, to have thought more fully about themselves and their world, they might have minimized the stress and avoided the waste and misery of having made inappropriate choices.

Reflexivity and Agency

I want to end this review of psychological issues and processes by describing the two factors which need to be present, but are often absent, in male development.

The word 'reflexivity' has become part of our contemporary jargon. It means thought, but more that, it indicates depth of thought. It involves thinking about one's thinking, asking why you thought as you did. Let us take the example of career choice. Some youth will say that they have no idea about what they want to do. The first stage is for them to think of some possibilities. But in itself that is not enough. We noted the case of the boy who expressed the wish to enter medicine without recognizing the GCE A level requirements and the length of time he would have to spend in higher education. The next level of thought involves learning about the requirements and characteristics of a particular career. Another level is to acquire some self-knowledge, to recognize one's own abilities, interests and temperament. Only if there is a reasonable match between what one can offer and what a career demands is there a good possibility of success. In other aspects of identity development reflexivity may be extended further, to ponder the meaning of life, or one's personal values, in order to identify a satisfying lifestyle. I am not being so naive as to suggest that all young men should be locked into the task of understanding abstract ideologies, but am arguing that there is a need to go part of the way along the road to greater understanding.

People are naturally lazy and, without stimulus, may not engage in significant thought. The discourse of the male peer group rarely touches on profound issues. Given this need to undergo a degree of reflexivity in order to achieve a satisfactory sense of identity, then it rests with adults to provide the stimulus. We need to create the opportunities for discussion in which the youth can have their ideas challenged and lack of knowledge addressed. Adults can provide such stimulus indirectly merely by providing alternative role models, giving access to different beliefs and lifestyles, but within schools some formal provision within Personal and Social Education may be required.

Thought alone solves very little. Having acquired some sense of what they are like, and what they want to do, the young men need next a sense of agency. 'Agency' is another jargon term. To sociologists it deals with the practical means a social group can pursue to realize their aims. Marxist thought, for example, describes how the weakness of individual members of the proletariat can be overcome by banding together in collective action. This joining together provides the means or agency.

Psychologists are more concerned with subjective feelings rather than social actions. To us agency is essentially about the individual having a belief that he can do something to realize his ambitions. He does not simply see himself as being a victim of circumstances, tossed like a cork on the sea of social forces, but having some control over his fate. Talking to young men, particularly among those from working-class homes and some ethnic minorities, one cannot fail to be struck by their lack of sense of agency. Many see themselves trapped in an unenviable position. Even if they have ambitions and hopes they have no idea how to realize them. Again the poverty of discourse within the peer group is part of the problem.

Two of the qualities of psychological competence in an adult are empathy and self-knowledge. Empathy for others, of different age, gender, class or race, provides the basis for living and working with others in the community. Self-knowledge, of both cognitive and affective qualities, of beliefs and desires, provides the foundation for entering both work and personal relationships. Neither empathy nor self-knowledge grow spontaneously through maturation, but have to be acquired, initially by reflexivity, and then by learning how to realize one's hopes and ambitions. The young have to gain both the competence and confidence to undertake this process.

6   What is New?

Although it was accepted in the opening chapter of this book that there may be a degree of media exaggeration in the reporting of the male malaise, there remains solid evidence that both the recent academic achievement and behaviour of young men gives cause for concern. Some of the possible causal factors, such the biological disposition of males, have presumably not changed in recent years. In this event, what has changed? As with most social developments the movement probably becomes a coincidence of factors. Some of these have already been mentioned. For example, the improvements in health care mean that far more boys survive infancy, so that men are now in a majority in many age-groups. Between 1949 and 1995 the number of deaths of children and young people in this country was cut by 80 per cent. In the former year the commonest cause was premature birth, responsible for 5,569 deaths, in the latter year it was road accidents, causing 533 deaths. Knowing the extent to which men have become socialized into adulthood through a steady relationship with a woman, the existence of more unattached males might promote a more widespread 'laddish' culture.

Changes in the Labour Market

Possibly the single most important influence has been the change in the labour market. Since about 1980 there has been a drastic loss of jobs in industries which have traditionally employed men, particularly unskilled or partially-skilled males. In the period 1981–96 over 400,000 jobs were lost in both mining and the metal working industries in Britain, and over 300,000 in both transport and construction. These losses were matched with an increase in excess of 900,000 jobs in computer-related work, 450,000 in social work, 334,000 in hotels and restaurants and 247,000 in education. Two things are evident when we compare the two lists. Many of the new posts have been created in fields demanding skills or where higher education is a necessary qualification. It is also true that these new careers are not dependent on male muscular strength and are therefore open equally well to women. The net result, as noted in Chapter 1, is that unemployment is particularly common among unskilled young men.

The problem is exacerbated by two contexts in which these men seem to be very inflexible. The first is in what they regard as proper work for men. They see mining or manufacturing as providing work which confirms their masculinity, while working in an office would undermine this sense of self. So, even if work is available in the community they may be reluctant to enter such employment.

The dilemma is that of the irresistible force meeting the irremovable object. The fixed object is the male prejudice about types of employment. The irresistible force is that of social change. It is true that the British government in the 1980s might have alleviated some of the social stress, by allowing the rundown of traditional manufacturing industries to occur more slowly. However, regardless of what any government could have done, the long-term effects would be the same. We live in a global market, where costs are reduced either through the use of new technology to replace many jobs or through locating labour-intensive work in the low-cost areas of South East Asia or East Europe. There is no viable scenario in which the former jobs in mining and manufacturing can be recreated. In this event young men either have to change their aspirations or face the prospect of extended periods of unemployment.

Obviously there are social and geographical variables. In some parts of Britain the tradition has been for 90 per cent of the male population to work in coal mining. Once the mines were closed there were two problems; there were few alternative forms of employment and the labour force had no experience of working, or even envisaging working, in other fields. In one well-known housing estate in north-east England 70 per cent of the families have no-one in employment.

The second expression of inflexibility is how males tend to envisage work within their life. In recent decades women have succeeded in becoming increasingly flexible, exercising the choice to prioritize a career or the family, to work full or part time. If there is a lack of work for males then the men might adapt by altering the dynamics within the family, so that the husband and wife assume equal responsibility for earning money and also for the care of the house and family. It is precisely among unskilled men that the greatest reluctance to take on these latter responsibilities is most apparent. The effects can be seen by looking at which parents visit schools for informal discussions about their child's progress. Fathers very rarely attend on their own. One study found that among the better-educated parents, measured by the mother having at least GCE A levels, the commonest arrangement is for both parents to participate (51 per cent) and in only 38 per cent of the cases did the mother have to attend on her own. With the less well-educated parents in only 26 per cent of the cases did both parents participate and for 69 per cent of the time it was the mother on her own (West et al., 1998).

My own work with adolescents reveals that the majority of boys still believe that the man in the family should be the primary wage earner. They still see that as their role yet at the same time they are taking very few steps to realize it. They are working less diligently and successfully at academic subjects than their female peers and, as noted earlier, they have less clear and precise career plans. These contradictions are likely to inhibit them finding some resolution to their problems.

The effects are not solely practical, in terms of gaining an income, but also impact on self-image and self-esteem. In the middle of the twentieth century, when perhaps three-quarters of men were still in the top half of the national earnings table, men could take pride in their financial contribution to the family. If now they neither make such a contribution, nor assume a major responsibility for child care, then it can reasonably asked, what are they contributing to society? Terms such as 'the redundant male', have entered contemporary discourse.

The anthropologist, Margaret Mead, summed up the traditional situation:

> In every known society, the male's need for achievement can be recognized. Men may cook, or weave or dress dolls or hunt humming-birds, but if such activities are appropriate occupations for men, then the whole society, men and women alike, votes them as important. When the same occupations are performed by women, they are regarded as less important. In a great number of human societies, men's sureness of their sex role is tied up with their right, or ability, to practice some activity that women are not allowed to practice.
>
> (Mead, 1962: 157–8)

In the light of these words we can appreciate the extent of social change which has overtaken us in recent decades.

The evidence from psychology is that career has been the main anchor upon which males fix their sense of personal identity. Willott and Griffin report:

> Talk of masculinity, for men in our study, tended to be anchored to ideas about getting out of the house and bringing home a sufficient amount of money to be independent of the state. Unemployment served to undermine hegemonic masculinities at various 'sites', especially the home and the pub ... the contradictions associated with being white and male (and therefore powerful) but also working class and unemployed are complex and profound.
>
> (1996: 89)

The effects of long-term unemployment have been extensively studied. In the short term it is the middle-aged man who is made redundant after a career in full-time unemployment who suffers most. He suddenly encounters a loss of income, a loss of status and the need to adjust to a different pattern of living (Super, 1957; Fryer and Ullah, 1987). For youth, who have yet to enter employment, the short-term effects are not too dramatic, as they do not experience a loss of income and their status is little different from those still undergoing full-time education. However, the longer-term effects are more damaging, with the loss of confidence and wish to work leading to depression and anomie (Winefield et al., 1993).

Willis (1977) pointed out that the less academic boys tended to muck around at school, not taking the teachers and work really seriously, until the prospect of employment approached. Entry into the world of work imposed a discipline on the youth. They now had to be at work on time, contribute fully to the activity, and cooperate with their work mates. In this way they were becoming socialized into one part of adult living and without employment no such socialization occurs.

The Lack of Male Mentors

We saw in Chapter 3 that the psychological task for the young boy is to dis-identify with his mother and begin to identify with males. Clearly, the father is usually the crucial player in this process. The change in this context relates to the high divorce rates and instability of marriage. In 1995 in Britain there were a total of 322,000 marriages, of which 192,000 were first marriages, and there were also 155,000 divorces (Office for National Statistics, 1998). Assuming that the present patterns continue we can predict that over 40 per cent of all marriages will end in divorce. Boys seem particularly damaged by this process, possibly because mothers commonly have custody of the children. About 20 per cent of families with dependent children are being brought up by a mother on her own and about 1 per cent by the father. In about 40 per cent of the cases where the mother has custody the father loses all contact with his children within two years of the divorce.

What these figures reveal is that a considerable minority of boys are now being brought up without the socializing influence of a father being at home. Not only does a father serve as a role model, a demonstration of what masculinity involves, but traditionally the father has had a major disciplinary role as well. The tendency of boys to take risks and challenge authority has been balanced by adult males, including fathers, teachers and the police, exercising constraints. What we commonly now witness is a breakdown of the authority systems. Other adult males can largely replace the father, but, as noted earlier, there has been a loss of contexts, such as youth clubs and the scouts, in which male mentors might be met.

The current position is full of paradoxes. Noting the loss of fathers in many families, there has been some public voice calling for more men to enter primary school teaching to act as mentors. In direct contradiction to this plan many primary schools are now reluctant to allow male students undertake teaching practice with them for fear of child abuse. The degree of concern was captured by the front page headline in *The Times Educational Supplement* of 26 August 1998: 'Pervert label puts men off teaching'. Some parents are arguing that if a man enters primary teaching he must have a sexual motivation and recognition of this belief may deter a young man entering the profession.

The overall effect is that the lack of guidance from adult males makes the process of growing into adulthood that much more confusing and difficult for young men.

Consumerism

Another factor which contributes to the sense of instability in the young has been the rise of consumerism. Not all youth have the financial resources to be involved. High levels of unemployment, the cuts in student grants and in social provision for 16–18-year-olds have all made the lot of many young men much harder. Yet, a sizeable proportion of the population have enough income surplus to their immediate basic needs to indulge in spending for leisure and pleasure. Among youth this trend is seen in the purchase of designer clothes, including trainers, compact discs and computers, and in going to clubs and similar social outlets. Perhaps the most striking transformation has been in football, with its emergence into a multi-million pound part of an entertainment industry, while at the same time schools and local authorities have had to dispose of their playing fields.

Consumerism is not only expressed through the purchase of objects but also in adopting particular lifestyles, ranging from holidays to a greater concern with the body image. Parker writes:

> The body has been ever present within the marketing orbits of mass consumption, and has come to represent the central focus of consumer culture today. Its worth rests not in its autonomous development, but in its ability to match popular ideals of youth, health fitness and beauty. ... such vast number of people have become preoccupied with issues of health and physical appearance, once-trivialized notions of 'keep fit' now constitute the corner-stone of a multi-million dollar fitness industry.
>
> (1996b: 129–30)

The Canadian sociologist James Cote argues that consumerism is a symptom of a fundamentally new form of social organization. 'Social-identity formation is postulated to differ in each type of society, such that according to the particular cultural prototype it tends to be *ascribed* in pre-modern societies, *achieved* in early-modern societies, and *managed* in late-modern ones' (1996: 420). In essence, he is arguing that in older cultures the young had little choice and their position in society was determined by place and birth. In the growth of industrialized societies entrepreneurism allowed the individual the opportunity to achieve financial and social success. In contemporary society, he is arguing, the young express their individuality through image-management.

Although in some respects I find this argument persuasive, it does leave open the psychological aspects. Consumerism implies the pursuit of fashion, something which is short term. Creating an image of oneself which conforms to the current fashion does nothing to give the youngster a sense of continuity or coherence of the self. The essential requirement for successful living is to achieve an appropriate balance between flexibility and steadfastness. In dealing with the external world, such as in seeking employment, one needs to be flexible. In maintaining psychic equilibrium one needs to maintain some reasonably consistent self-image and sense of identity. If Cote is correct in his analysis, then the young seem to be failing to get this right, being inflexible in their notions of employment, but fickle in their sense of self.

Drugs

The situation with respect to the use of illegal drugs epitomizes many of the newly emerging issues in our societies. Some drug use has been recorded through the centuries, but until recently the young have been unable to afford to purchase drugs such as cannabis, cocaine or heroin. The growth in international trade has forced prices down and made these drugs widely available in our society. Most disturbingly there is evidence of dealers now targeting teenagers, by offering initial doses of crack cocaine free. Clearly, this is a calculated 'loss leader', offered in the belief that a potential customer is created, who either has the means to pay for the drugs or has to pay for it by stealing or prostitution.

Probably the most thorough research on drug use among the young was that of Miller and Plant (1996) who reported, for example, that 43.6 per cent of boys aged 15–16 admitted to having used cannabis. Almost certainly the figure will go up if we look at older teenagers and has probably increased since that research was carried out. Everyone working in this field whom I have met tells me that the majority of youth are now users of illegal drugs. My point is not to argue the rights and wrongs of the situation but to point out the gravity of the case where a majority of our youngsters are technically criminals. Within a democracy, laws work by gaining broad acceptance from the population, yet here we have the case where social stratification by age and consumerism have combined to make the existing laws unacceptable to the majority of an age cohort.

Despite the efforts of teachers in the field of social, personal and health education adults have failed to persuade the youth not to use drugs. One problem is that the resources of those engaged in drug-use prevention are minute compared to the resources of those involved in drug distribution. Another difficulty is that governments have oscillated in their responses, sometimes with some tolerance being shown, notably in the Netherlands but also in Britain with respect to being found with small amounts of drugs, and taking a tough line with all people found in possession. Overall, the young see a confused picture, in which adults use tobacco and alcohol, but condemn drugs such as cannabis which may be no more harmful, and where law enforcement is patchy and uncertain.

Feminism and the Backlash

Since the 1960s there have been immense social and legal changes for the betterment of women. Many former practices, such as discrimination within the workplace and setting quotas for undergraduate admissions to medical schools, have been outlawed. The women's movement has led to the creation of various groups, both for general support and also to meet some specific purposes, for example, with assertiveness training. Perhaps even more impressive has been the growth in feminist thinking which has now permeated and changed almost every field of academic study. Feminists have unpacked the processes of interaction between men and women which have traditionally led to a hegemony of masculinity. In looking more carefully at the role of women and at gender relations, feminist thought has inevitably challenged many preconceptions of men about themselves. The traditional biographies of men gave accounts of their achievements as a statesman, artist or scientist, but commonly said little about the emotional life of an individual. Men were assessed simply in the light of their achievements. The key question for men is how they should react to this process.

Horrocks, a psychotherapist, describes his findings:

> For the past two or three decades we have become used to feminism showing the damaging effects of gender inequality on women. It has often been assumed that men, in their positions of dominance, have the most exciting and rewarding careers, feel more powerful in their public and private lives, and are generally favoured over women. While there is clearly some cogency to these arguments, I have found in my work that in fact many men are haunted by feelings of emptiness, impotence and rage. They feel abused, unrecognized by modern society. While manhood offers compensations and prizes, it can also bring with it emotional autism, emptiness and despair.
>
> (1994: 1)

It must be noted that women have had to pay a price for their newly won freedoms. Many are having to cope with combining the traditional female role of mother and housekeeper with the male function of pursuing a career. Young women are also copying some of the less desirable male traits. Between 1949 and 1995 crime rates for young people trebled overall, but increased eleven-fold for girls.

Some men, particularly younger men, have welcomed the change in the social climate, gaining the title 'the New Man'. They see the process which opened wider opportunities for women as having a similar function for men, emancipating the young man from the stern male strictures of the past, particularly those aimed at men who deviated from the social norm. The problem for these individuals is that they recognize that they need to change, to move away from the traditional roles, but are less certain what they should now do. What does becoming a New Man involve?

It has to be said that they meet uncertain responses, not only from other men who may have much to lose if traditional gender roles are modified, but also from many women. Some more conservative women dismiss these men as wimps for failing to assert themselves in typical male ways. Among feminists some take a liberal stance, welcoming these men as allies with whom they can negotiate to produce a better society. Other, more radical, feminists argue that in a sex war there can be no neutrality and at the end of the day all men will support their own side. Working, as I do, in a university in central London, I come across many such men who are totally puzzled about how to behave. They believe their intentions to be good but do not know how to realize these intentions. Typical stories are that when they offer to help a woman in some way, such as carrying a suitcase, they are accused of being sexist in seeing the woman as being in need of help. From other men they might meet overt aggression and some spend much of their social life in gay circles, as they experience less hostility and aggression, even though they themselves are heterosexual. In other circumstances I might doubt their denial of homosexual interests, but their accounts are marked by a high degree of openness and honesty, so that I believe their denials to be true. So we have a contemporary dilemma, that of some of our more thoughtful, sensitive and caring young men are finding themselves marginalized.

Others have reacted to the advance of women and feminist thinking by adopting some form of reactionary position. At its crudest the intention is to reverse the changes of recent decades and reassert male supremacy. This stance is not only purely negative it is also totally unrealistic in at least two ways. It would be hard to imagine a society which, having nurtured notions of equity, suddenly abandoned these in order to pursue a policy of discrimination. Past discrimination was largely possible because it was not discussed; it was covert or was simply justified as being the natural order of things. Once the inequalities were exposed they were bound to be challenged. Second, a reactionary policy cannot be delivered for purely pragmatic reasons. If we want men to command higher wages by virtue of their greater muscle power we have to revert to industrial practices which use human labour in this way. Decades of technological innovation would have to be jettisoned. Much of the male reaction is trivial, consisting simply of generating a list of grievances, such as men having to wait to a later age to draw a pension. The obvious retort is that men tend to draw higher wages while in employment. Thus each side can produce an ever growing list of grievances, without anyone coming up with a constructive proposal.

One of the more subtle conservative positions has been taken by the American poet and writer Robert Bly (1990). In essence his argument is that in the feminized society men only have an image of themselves as it is created by women, and they have to find within themselves and the culture of men, their true self. My problem with Bly's work is that I find his analysis of issues interesting but his proposed remedies very dubious. Noting that in earlier times there existed a number of rituals by which young men were initiated into manhood by older men, he argues for a return to such practices. Hence we have the scenario of men sitting around a fire in a forest glade, beating drums, flying flags and confessing their feelings to each other. Ignoring the disturbing echo of Hitler Youth in such activities, they still have to be criticized as they do not connect to the contemporary reality of these men's lives. Rituals matter if they correspond to a real social change. One aspect of marriage is that it changes the legal position of the partners, so it is more than mere ritual even for those who do not subscribe to a religious affiliation. Initiation rites in many societies mark a distinct change in the status and work of the young. Boys might move from being seen as children, being in the care of women, to joining men in their work. Bly's rituals do not have such significance.

Bly's arguments are partly based on Jung's work, with an appeal to the male archetype as found in history and mythology. Some contemporary Jungians are disturbed by this use of analytical psychology and in particular Tacey has taken up the issue:

> Ever since Robert Bly's *Iron John: A Book About Men* burst upon the international scene, we have witnessed a veritable avalanche of Jungian or pseudo-Jungian texts which attempt to 'solve' the crisis of masculinity. But although this new tradition of 'mythopoetic' writing about men is often insightful, and always alert to the critical situation of contemporary masculinity, I find it largely unsatisfactory. ... It asks how men can recover their former balance, not how they can discover a new, post-patriarchal equilibrium.
>
> (1997: 2)

A reactionary stance solves nothing, at the most it can only reopen the problems women had to address in the past. The key need is for men to negotiate a new role for themselves which is consonant with contemporary society and values.

Part II

Addressing the Issues

7 Academic Achievement

Concerns about young men have been expressed under two broad headings. There is a long-established series of complaints about social behaviour, being disruptive in school, unreasonable in the home, truanting and delinquency. More recently the focus has shifted to reports of underachievement in school work. In essence these two aspects will commonly stem from the same causes. To take the more extreme cases, truancy or school exclusion will inevitably impact on school learning. Nevertheless, I have followed the convention by dividing the consideration of academic achievement from behavioural concerns, but the two chapters need to be read with reference to each other.

The evidence for the underachievement of boys was introduced in Chapter 1. In this chapter the intention is to dig deeper, into possible causes and possible remedies, including some reference to specific subjects within the curriculum.

Gender Differences in Abilities and Learning Styles

The argument that boys are somehow less able is probably suspect, as historically they fared better than girls, but the evidence merits scrutiny.

We cannot say much about measures of general intelligence, as intelligence tests have been constructed, by the selection of items in them, to yield the same mean values for males and females. What does emerge is that males tend to cluster less closely around the mean value than females, with more at both extreme ends of the scale. In psychometric language the scores for men show a larger standard deviation. This finding matches that of educational achievement. Although boys do less well at GCSE measured in terms of obtaining A to C grades, the difference is less if one looks solely at A grades. At the other end of the scale boys form a large majority of those diagnosed as having learning difficulties.

More relevant to the bulk of the population is a fairly consistent finding that boys show a greater aptitude for spatial and mathematical tasks and girls for those involving language. In the past literally hundreds of studies were made of such gender difference, e.g. Maccoby and Jacklin (1975), but

Hyde (1981) in a meta-analysis of all the data revealed that these differences are quite small, in the order of 0.2 of a standard mean difference. Such measured differences might account for small variations in achievement, with perhaps girls gaining 60 per cent of the better grades in English and only 40 per cent in science and mathematics. But as we saw earlier, the evidence shows greater differentials than this, both in the pass rates in such GCSE subjects as English and in participation rates in higher education. Whatever such aptitude tests reveal, whether it is a biological difference or something gained through the experience of schooling, it does little to explain educational differentials.

The concept of learning styles can be confusing, it describes a cognitive quality, but it may also be seen as a personality variable. In essence it is a preference for a particular way of thinking about an issue, even when alternative ways are possible. Style differs from aptitude in the sense that overall there is no right or wrong way, although in a specific context one mode of thinking might be more appropriate. Aptitudes can be seen as being one-way, starting from a zero position of having no competence and moving upwards with increasing ability. There is no benefit from not possessing an ability. Styles are usually postulated in bi-polar terms with each alternative conferring some advantages and some disadvantages.

Perhaps the best-known example of learning style refers to the field-dependent or holistic approach in contrast to the field-independent or analytical alternative. Someone with the latter preference tends to focus on one aspect of a problem, that part which is believed to be the crucial element. Such thinking can be seen when a car breaks down. There is only likely to be one cause of the malfunction so the need is to identify that cause. The contrast can be seen when one is considering the ecological or environmental effects of some change to the land. Removing a wood, for example, will have a series of knock-on effects, on drainage, animal and plant life, wind-cover and light penetration. To comprehend this range one has to see the whole picture and not ignore the wider context in evaluating an action.

There is evidence, including that of Gilligan (1982) already mentioned, that women tend to be more field dependent and men more field independent. This difference can be reflected in preferences for specific subjects, or task within subjects, and in assessment. As neither learning style confers overall advantage the need is to present curriculum material in ways which involve both.

Differences in the Approach to School Work

There is clear evidence that boys and girls approach their work in different ways. Long-established beliefs of teachers have been confirmed by the EOC/OFSTED (1996) publication of the findings of OFSTED inspectors. They are able to report on findings gathered from a large number of schools so such variables as social class and ethnicity should not distort the story. Some of their main findings are summarized below.

1 'more girls are now taking traditional boys' subjects ... although boys are still reluctant to take traditional girl's subjects ...' (p. 13). This finding confirms the inflexibility of many young men in dealing with a changing world.

2 'girls are more successful than boys in some of the more reflective aspects of work ...' (p. 17). Teachers commonly report that often boys plunge into an activity without adequate thought about what they are trying to do and at the end of the exercise fail to think through what the conclusions or implications might be.

3 'girls and boys have different approaches to planning and organizing their work. Girls are more likely to bring the right equipment to lessons and complete their homework diaries' (p. 17).

These three findings begin to build up a picture of some causes of male failure. Their reluctance to consider different school subjects parallels their reluctance to consider alternative forms of employment, or show tolerance to different forms of sexuality. Masculinity has to be confirmed by sticking closely to a particular model of what men are like and do. The lack of thought and organization must inhibit performance. There is no psychological evidence of these being innate qualities, so presumably these are consequences of the peer group culture, in which the swot is derided, and one should be 'cool' about school work. Boys cannot be seen to be taking this work too seriously.

Some remedial steps:

1 The lack of reflexivity, and the consequent carelessness, can be addressed by specific procedures. Students may have to produce a plan of action before actually beginning a task. They can be given examples of careless work, e.g. containing spelling and grammatical errors and have to correct them. This activity should cause them to review their own work more carefully. It is noteworthy that the cognitive acceleration programmes involve the students having to identify variables and plan their actions before commencing a task (Adey et al., 1995).

2 Boys seem to benefit from having well established routines and rules, otherwise they tend to be disorganized. Tasks need to be clearly spelt out, e.g. on a worksheet, and the teacher has to set consistent rules about what the students must bring with them to the lessons.

Coeducation and Class Management

The major move towards coeducation in Britain in the 1960s went alongside the comprehensive school developments as part of the growth of inclusive educational provision. Specifically, four claims were made for coeducation.

1   *Equity* It was believed that often the education of boys had been taken more seriously than that of girls, so that boys' schools had better teachers and resources. Most of those within the feminist movement at that time supported the move towards coeducation.
2   *Economy* Certain subject groups, for example physics in girls' schools and a second modern language for boys, tended to be too small to be economical. A coeducational school gave viable groups across a wide range of curriculum subjects. In some fields, such as music and drama, having a mixed school population conferred immense advantages.
3   *Social education* It was argued that boys and girls have to relate and work together as adults and these processes would be easier if they were educated together. Coeducation provided a more natural site for social development.
4   *School discipline* Boys were seen to be the more disruptive and more ready to challenge authority and fail to engage in school work. The presence of girls might minimize these problems and the girls might learn to be more assertive and confident in having to work alongside the boys.

Within a decade, or so, some feminists (e.g. Deem, 1984; Mahony, 1985) were having second thoughts, arguing that the male dominance of the curriculum, what was taught and how it was taught, was complete in coeducational schools. Within girls' schools women teachers could modify content and methods enough to make the lessons more relevant and accessible to girls.

Despite these concerns, mixed schools are very much the norm in most parts of Europe and North America, except for schools with a religious affiliation, and educationists in these countries express surprise that the issue is still being debated in Britain.

It is interesting to note what the EOC/OFSTED report said on the British situation:

> An analysis of inspection reports suggests that the quality of education in single-sex and mixed schools reflects well-established differences in the performance and attitudes of girls and boys. In other words, the fact that girls generally have more positive attitudes than boys, and achieve higher standards, is a significant factor in the relative success of schools. Therefore, in almost all areas covered by the *Framework for Inspection*, girls' schools are generally found to perform best, mixed schools next, and boys' schools least effectively.
>
> (1996: 24)

This comment, confirming many research findings, has led to the proposal that we need mixed schools for boys and single-sex schools for girls! This paradox should not be taken as a condemnation of the research, but as indicating that research often serves to clarify the questions rather than provide answers. What can we make of this finding? At one level the argument can be reduced to asking which sex is sacrificed by the choice of schooling system. Nevertheless, the weight of arguments for coeducation listed previously, and its widespread success throughout most of the developed world, suggests that it provides the better option. In this event, the key issue is to manage mixed schools to ensure the maximum advantage for all.

To take one example, we know that girls tend to be more thoughtful and careful in undertaking their work, while the boys rush in. If the pupils in a mixed school work within single-sex groups, and they usually will if allowed to do so, then each group will tend to continue in the gender-stereotyped way. Nothing has been gained by having the mix. If boys and girls are forced to work within mixed groups then the girls might be able to inject more thought and care into the work. This desired outcome may not happen if the boys are allowed to use their more aggressive style of talking to dominate the proceedings. In other words, two things are required for successful working: having the pupils in mixed groups, and ensuring that the discussion within groups is such that the girls are allowed to participate fully.

Similarly, girls will tend to have a wider vocabulary, a more sophisticated command of syntax, and put more thought into their arguments. Consequently, their speech is likely to raise the level of discourse in the classroom. But this desired outcome will not occur if the more confident and talkative boys shut the girls out of the discussion. Teachers have to manage the classroom dynamics to ensure the best learning environment.

Gender and Academic Failure

In some respects it proves more useful in analysing learning processes to look at failure rather than success. If pupils are successful, and assuming we are not witnessing cheating or good luck, then we can say little about the process. If students fail then we can seek to diagnose what went wrong. In that sense failure can be informative.

To make an analysis of where boys might go wrong I am using a simple taxonomy. We know that success depends both on being able to do the task, the cognitive aspect, and being willing to do it, the affective aspect. Second, I am dividing the learning task into three stages, starting the work, carrying out the work and providing the required answer or outcome. We can identify likely gender differences in both the cognitive and affective aspects in all three stages.

Stage 1 The cognitive demand at this stage is for the pupils to understand what they have been asked to do. Boys are notoriously poor listeners and are less likely to have listened with adequate care to the instructions. They are likely to start doing anything which has some relevance to the task even if it does not directly address the issue. Girls are more likely to agree among themselves precisely what they have to do before actually starting the work.

The affective problem at this stage is that the student may assume that he or she cannot cope with the task. Girls are less likely to possess adequate confidence to proceed and can slip into a cycle of learned helplessness in which lack of effort leads to failure, which, in turn, reinforces the initial lack of confidence.

Stage 2 The cognitive demands include possessing adequate initial knowledge and skills to undertake the work. Much of school learning is linear, in which mastering a new concept is dependent on having already mastered a number of previous ideas. As boys tend to take less care in making sure they do understand things they may find themselves disadvantaged at this stage. This point will be expanded on later in this chapter in dealing with the learning of mathematics.

The affective issues at this stage involve a lack of motivation so that the student loses interest or is easily distracted. The consequent inadequate effort is likely to lead to failure. There are probably only minor gender differences in respect to this area. The lesser confidence of girls is likely to be compensated for by a greater willingness to engage with work set by a teacher.

Stage 3 The cognitive problem is that the student may not know how to express the answer or finding in an acceptable form. One example is in foreign language lessons when students are asked to provide the translation of an English word within the context of a complete sentence in the other language. Boys will tend to be impulsive and shout out the translation of the single word, failing to comply with the instruction relating to a sentence.

The affective barrier at this stage is that the pupil may know the correct answer but be reluctant to give it for fear of being wrong. This fear is more common among girls who try to avoid censure or public humiliation by remaining mute. Boys are more likely to proffer an answer even if it is only a guess.

Looking back at this analysis it can be seen that both genders tend to have some specific areas of weaknesses, although overall the boys are likely to do less well. The pedagogic task is to recognize all these possible problems and seek to minimize the effects of each.

Assessment

It is a common illusion that there exists some fair and foolproof assessment procedure. For example, when I was teaching in an American high school I was only allowed to assess students through the use of multiple-choice tests. The underlying rationale for this ruling is that it removed any element of teacher bias or prejudice from the assessment. The reality is that no one assessment procedure alone serves all functions.

Depending on which qualities we wish to reward we can change the assessment format, but in so doing it is likely that the relative gender success will also be affected. Murphy (1980) describes the effects of changing a GCE O level geography examination by introducing a multiple-choice component. Hitherto the boys and girls had enjoyed equal success but the new format lead to about 10 per cent more boys gaining A to C grades than the girls.

There is now sufficient evidence for examiners to predict the likely gender differential for different formats and even specific items within a given format. The reader is referred to other texts, e.g. Gipps and Murphy (1994), for details, but some major features can be summarized.

Boys tend to do better in providing short answers (of the right/wrong form), at providing explanations for effects, and with practical tests. Girls tend to do better with extended writing, at looking at an issue from a variety of perspectives, in other words exercising empathy, and in working with literary material. There are some further variations within this pattern. Boys generally do well with multiple-choice items with the exception of those which have a complicated stem. If, for example, a question starts with this instruction, 'Which of the following is not an example of ... ' then the evidence suggests that some boys fail to notice the word *not* and give an incorrect response. The common error of boys of rushing into the task and consequently making careless mistakes is thus revealed.

Another weakness for boys is in the production of course work which has to be done outside class time. Presumably the girls are more conscientious while the boys spend less time in their evenings in doing homework. It has been argued that the apparent decline of boys' achievement in recent years is solely a product of changes in the examinations. It is true that a decline in the boys' performance set in about the time that GCSE, with its greater prominence for course work, replaced the GCE O level. However, this factor cannot be the sole explanation. By government edict in 1992 the amount of credit given for course work was reduced yet the relative decline of the boys' performance has continued since then.

A sophisticated view of assessment procedures suggests that different forms of testing address different aspects of performance and that only the use of a variety of test forms yields anything approximating to a balanced or fair outcome. It is also arguable that different tests work best for different subjects within the curriculum. Commonly, teachers of English like the use of course work for assessment while teachers of mathematics prefer more traditional examinations. The key message for us in looking at gender differences in academic work is scrutinize with care the evidence being offered to us.

Language and Literacy

In reviewing the achievement of boys within specific areas of the curriculum nothing is more striking, or more important, than the position in language-based subjects. In the 1996 GCSE examinations 40.1 per cent of the boys and 57.7 per cent of the girls achieved A to C grades. Moving on to modern languages, 26.4 per cent of the boys and 41.3 per cent of the girls achieved A to C grades in any one such language. These GCSE results are only part of a life-long pattern. Girls do better at English at all the Key Stages earlier in the school. Twice as many girls take A level English and females make up 70 per cent of full-time undergraduates in the language based fields.

There is some evidence of brain function differences in respect to language, with women using both hemispheres and men being more dependent on one. However, this finding alone does not account for the educational differences, as the same brain characteristics are found in handling spatial tasks, and in this instance boys tend to be better. The fact that girls receive more talk in infancy will reinforce any innate biological bias. Additionally, as already noted, the discourse within male peer groups tends to be limited, with the group respecting a willingness for action rather than verbal openness.

Whatever the causes of the boys' poorer development there can be no mistaking its importance. Obviously command of language, including literacy, is essential for communication both within many jobs and everyday social life. The fact that boys make up 80 per cent of those classified as suffering from Moderate Learning Difficulties is largely a reflection of their poor literacy. Language is not only important for communication but for thinking itself. To a considerable extent we think with language, so an impoverished command of language inhibits sophisticated thinking. Although we might now regard Bernstein's original distinction between restricted and extended codes for speech as being somewhat simplistic, the broader thesis remains valid: language is a tool with which we think.

The boys' deficiency in both oral and written language skills has received considerable attention, including OFSTED (1993), the QCA (1998) and various individual writers, e.g. Millard (1997). From such sources a clear picture emerges. The EOC/OFSTED report summarizes the evidence:

> secondary age boys tend to have more negative attitudes towards reading and writing than girls. They often have narrower experiences of fiction, write more predictably, and have difficulty with affective aspects of English. Their learning process improves when the teaching convinces them of the value of what they are doing ...
>
> (1996: 16)

Given the importance of literacy as a foundation for nearly all learning, we can appreciate why the government has set up the National Literacy Project with the idea of a Literacy Hour every day in primary schools.

Modern language education suffers because many boys cannot perceive its value. There is some justification in this attitude in so far as much international business is carried out in English, including the handling of air traffic and the production of civil engineering contracts. Ambitious boys wishing to work in these fields in other countries have to acquire some competence in English as part of their professional training. Nevertheless, proficiency in languages still conveys advantages to those in Britain, particularly in the context of the European Union, and the boys have failed to recognize the cultural advantages which might be gained.

Boys tend to spend little time reading from choice. Millard (1997) found in a research study that boys aged eight to 14 mainly only read in school while girls do most of their reading at home. Boys read little within the commonly accepted canon of good literature, and when they do read fiction they do so for different motives. Millard writes:

> It was certainly the case that boys and girls not only chose different kinds of fiction but they were oriented to receive the same books in different ways. Boys read with an eye at finding out new information, even from their fiction; girls enjoyed the dissection of relationships.
>
> (1997: 160)

Millard also found that the two genders read different magazines. Boys' interests were almost entirely in computer and football magazines while girls were as strongly biased towards teen culture, i.e. magazines specifically written for girls of this age. Boys also tend to read technical manuals relating to some leisure interests, material, including biographies, about sports and sportsmen, and humorous articles. One problem is that the texts they read are not always well written. One of the strengths of the writers of fiction read by boys in previous generations, by authors such as John Buchan and Conan Doyle, is they could combine vigorous narrative with a good literary style. Given this bias, should we encourage reading by giving boys more factual texts, or will that perpetuate their poverty of emotional expression? And should we force fiction on them, to open up the areas of feelings to discussion ?

Not only is the content of boys' reading limited but they read in a specific way, episodically, picking out bits of information which interest them and not pursuing a reading of a continuous narrative. Consequently, they do not encounter material in which plot and character can be built up with elaboration and subtlety.

When asked to justify their lack of reading, boys will commonly describe it as boring. In part this may be true, reflecting their liking for more active pursuits, but probably for many the underlying reason is that their reading skills are so limited that the process proves too difficult and laborious to be enjoyable.

Boys tend to have difficulty in constructing narratives, so given a piece of blank paper they are slow in generating a piece of continuous prose. If some structure is provided for them, for example by being given a couple of opening sentences to start the essay then they seem to cope more satisfactorily. Similarly, they fare better with exercises requiring short answers. Overall they seem to find writing tedious, possibly because both their handwriting and spelling may be poor, and are happier when they can use a word-processor. The use of the technology appeals to them but, additionally, it overcomes the problem of poor handwriting and makes corrections to spelling a relatively painless exercise.

Punter and Burchell (1996) questioned the GCSE English examiners for one examination board. Of twenty characteristics of student writing girls were seen to do better with fifteen, including writing extended pieces, writing answers to open-ended questions, showing awareness of the intended audience and showing awareness of character motivation. Boys were seen to be better in only three areas, writing short notes, writing factually and interpreting visual material, such as lists of data and diagrams.

In the light of all these findings we can summarize the steps that can be taken to improve language and literacy skills of boys as follows:

1   They must read, as competence, confidence and interest, can only be gained through experience. Setting aside time within school hours for reading is an essential starting point.
2   We can try to identify suitable 'non-literary texts' which might stimulate their interest, i.e. books which may be outside the common canon of good literature, but still possess some literary merit. Some biographies or accounts of adventure could come into this category. School libraries should contain suitable texts and pupils can be given reading lists to help them select items in public libraries and bookshops.
3   Slow readers probably need one-to-one help. Either peer tutoring or a scheme involving parents might be considered for providing the necessary manpower.

4 Their interest in computer technology can be harnessed, both by allowing word-processing for some of their school work and also encouraging their interest in the Internet. One of the advantages of the latter medium is that it forces the participant to write.
5 Classroom discussions allow students to practice the articulation of their ideas. If they find it difficult to move beyond the repetition of simple assertions then help can be given by providing participants with outlines of some ideas and arguments they may wish to develop. Once again it seems the case that boys need a structure in which to work.
6 They need to learn to listen with care and avoid the situation in which they seize on one point which interests them and miss or confuse the rest of the passage. Listening skills can be developed through formal exercises in which they have to write a precis or verbally summarize something which they have just heard.
7 As noted earlier, a relatively easy way of directing their attention to the need to check for spelling and grammatical errors is to give them a passage, either on paper or a computer, which contains a number of such errors which they have to correct. It seems that the act of writing their own text is so unpleasant that they cannot summon up the effort to re-read it looking for errors. Correcting material which has already been written appeals more.
8 If they find writing continuous prose difficult then some help can be given by providing an opening sentence, or some other structuring device.

The key to all these proposals is that reading, writing, listening and speaking skills can only be developed through practice. They do not develop spontaneously through maturation. Hence our task is to provide opportunities for such practice. Not all can be done within the lessons allocated to English and both a whole-school policy and the involvement of parents are needed.

Mathematics

This subject is one in which boys have traditionally performed better than girls, although the difference has been less than that in the physical sciences. In the 1988 GCSE examination 38.9 per cent of the boys and 33.1 per cent of the girls obtained A to C grades. Since that time the girls have been steadily gaining ground so that in 1996 the figure for girls had reached 40.9 per cent and for boys was 39.7 per cent. At the GCE A level the boys are still in a majority and in 1996 they made up 62 per cent of those entering university to study mathematics.

In the recent past the relatively poor performance by girls led to a number of initiatives to address the issue and make the subject more girl-friendly (e.g. Burton, 1986). As late as 1989 the Department of Education and

Science produced a booklet *Girls Learning Mathematics* (DES, 1989), which was based on the findings of inspection of schools, to recommend procedures to enhance the achievement of girls.

Part of the problem is that mathematics, like science, tends to have a masculine image, so it is seen to be more appropriate a field of study for boys than for girls. Some of the initiatives to encourage more girls into mathematics addressed this factor. However, the gender issues are more complex than this one influence.

One striking feature emerging from research in mathematics education is that performance seems to be more strongly influenced by affective factors than in most other subjects. A new technical term, *mathophobia*, has been coined to describe a widespread, extreme fear of the subject. Some students find the prospect of working through a page of mathematical equations so alien an experience that they fail to engage with the task. It is not solely a matter of competence, as many students admit to me having this fear to some extent, even though if they make the effort to work through the material line-by-line they can understand it. The problem is seen to be so extensive and important a psychometric measure, the Mathematics Anxiety Rating Scale (Suin et al., 1972), has been developed to measure the quality among students.

We might predict that this phobic reaction affects males and females differently. Callaghan (1971), found that girls more commonly agreed with statements such as 'I am afraid of doing word problems' or 'I don't feel sure of myself in math' while the other major gender difference was that boys agreed with the idea that 'I like math because it is practical'. Girls seem to be more prone to self-doubt and learned helplessness and are thus vulnerable to failure unless the mathematics is made comprehensible to them. Boys are more likely to be concerned with success than understanding. They are more likely to be confident that they could cope if they had to, but in the meantime lack the motivation to do much.

The interesting thing about this predication is that it is confirmed by the more recent research findings of Boaler (1997a, 1997b). She looked at the response of secondary school pupils to different modes of mathematics teaching. Some teachers follow a traditional style in which they demonstrate how to carry out a mathematical operation and then set the pupils the task of carrying out a set of similar operations. Little or no explanation is given of why the process is important nor are the students expected to understand the mathematical significance of the task. Girls tend to dislike this situation, as they seek to understand what they are doing before they engage with the work. Boys can be motivated by competing with each other to race through the work to see who can finish first. Boys seem to be more ready to settle for knowing how to do something without knowing why they do it.

Other teachers move more slowly in taking care to explain what the operation means before asking the students to carry it out. The girls are much happier with this approach and perform as well, if not better, than the boys. In comparing the effects of the two teaching styles it can be seen that in the immediate short-term boys may perform better in the first example. However, further study of mathematics may demand an understanding of the mathematics already encountered in the curriculum, in which event the latter teaching style might prove to be better.

This work not only elucidates the different gender response to the mode of mathematics teaching but has implications for all concerned with education in this field. It raises the more fundamental question of what teachers are trying to achieve in this subject. In respect to the academic achievement of boys it raises the concern that they may learn in such a way that they enjoy initial success but later on discover that they have a shaky foundation for undertaking more advanced studies.

Science and Technology

Like mathematics, science has traditionally been an area of boys' strength, particularly in the physical sciences. Again, the story has been of girls catching up and overtaking the boys, so that in 1996 35.6 per cent of the girls and 33.0 per cent of the boys gained A to C grades in GCSE double science. Only a minority of students, about 7 per cent, take any of the single sciences, and here the boys do better overall. Men dominate the university intake in physics with 81 per cent of the cohort and with 62 per cent in chemistry. In biology women are in a majority, making up 55 per cent of the undergraduates.

As with mathematics, there were a number of initiatives in the 1970s and 1980s to enhance the performance of girls in science, which are described by Harding (1986) and Kelly (1987). More recently Kenway and Gough (1998) argued that little has changed and science is still largely construed in a masculine way. Research has failed to reveal sufficient cognitive differences to account for the lack of girls entering the physical sciences and their dearth has been attributed to other factors, such as the masculine image of the subject. Very few school students, boys or girls, could name an eminent female scientist other than Madame Curie. It was also argued that boys acquire a greater familiarity with science through their toys and games, so enter school science with both greater confidence and competence. Johnson and Murphy (1986) reported findings from the national assessment of performance survey which revealed that boys had considerably more experience outside school in using batteries, magnets, lenses, compasses and microscopes.

Another factor involved in opting for science turned out to be the personality of the student. Many decades ago work on eminent male scientists by Roe (1952) and Terman (1955) demonstrated that they not only possessed the expected cognitive strengths but also showed characteristic personality traits. The particular qualities are best summed up by Kubie: 'The young scientist often reaches maturity after a lopsided early development. ... If success rewards his consolatory scholarly efforts during adolescence, he may in later years tend to cultivate intellectual activity exclusively' (1954: 104).

Similarly Mitroff et al. wrote:

> Science, both as a characteristic method of obtaining knowledge and as a characteristic body of knowledge, has not only emphasised but glorified disinterested objectivity. ... What has not been so readily appreciated is that it has extracted a social cost from its silent partners ... science is deeply dependent upon women for the care and management of its affective or emotional life.
>
> (1977: 303–7)

These findings with professional scientists have been echoed in large-scale surveys of undergraduates (e.g. Entwistle and Wilson, 1977) and by myself with secondary school students (Head, 1980, 1985). The characteristics of many of the young men choosing science, being emotionally reticent, liking certainty and showing a degree of dogmatism, are typical authoritarian qualities of those who foreclose on their identity. A young man facing the emotional turbulence of adolescence might find the emotionally neutral field of science with its masculine image offering an appealing career and thus forecloses on this option.

There are two problems resulting from such foreclosure. For the individual the difficulty may arise when he realizes that he made an unsuitable choice and he then either has to continue with a degree of unhappiness or change direction. The drop-out rates among science students reveal a tendency to opt for the latter alternative. The second difficulty is for science itself. If an undue proportion of professional scientists are foreclosed males then their manner and behaviour is likely to strengthen the macho image of the subject. In other words, a self-perpetuating cycle might be set up with the image influencing recruitment. Easlea (1983) has taken the argument further, showing that the scientists developing nuclear weapons in the 1940s seemed to revel in their task and in 1945 were worried that the war might end before they had an opportunity to use the second bomb at Nagasaki. Interest in the scientific challenges had squeezed out any concern for the victims of such bombs. He argued:

> the nuclear arms race is in large underwritten by masculine behaviour. ... What, of course, makes masculine science particularly dangerous, as opposed to masculine prescientific magic and ritual, is that science truly 'works', that it really is efficacious, and therefore for the first time in history provides power over nature but provides it for men who are, to say the very least, humanly ill-equipped to make wise use of that power.
>
> (1983: 5)

I am not arguing that all male physical scientists foreclosed on their career choice, but that enough have done so to affect the image and conduct of science. Women may also foreclose, but they will do so by taking up careers with a feminine image.

There is a link between personality of young women and their response to science. Head and Ramsden (1990) conducted an experiment in which the secondary school teaching of physics was modified to make it more girl-friendly. The use of the science, its social and applied applications were stressed. Not only did more girls experiencing the new course opt to continue their studies of physics but the use of a psychometric personality measure revealed that a wider spectrum of personality types were attracted to the subject. In other words, the modified physics course yielded both quantitative and qualitative changes in the girls continuing their education in this field.

The dilemma for those involved in science education is whether the physical sciences should be left alone, as they are one of the few areas in which boys do relatively well, or should reforms be pursued even if boys then become disenchanted.

The situation with biological science is very different. The humanitarian potential seems to appeal to girls and young women. In early secondary school years boys say that the most interesting topics in science are rockets, motors, chemistry and computers, while girls choose health, child care and pets. Among undergraduates women are in a slight majority in medical schools, and a considerable majority in professions linked to medicine, such as nursing and psychology. It might be noted that fields favoured by men, engineering and the physical science, are those where jobs have not expanded to the same extent as in the fields linked to health.

With technology a curious situation exists. At the undergraduate level the male dominance continues, with men making up 85 per cent of the population. However, with Design and Technology in secondary schools the story is very different, with 13.3 per cent of the female year cohort gaining GCSE A to C grades, compared with 9.7 per cent for the boys. Two factors seem to explain the recent emergence of girls in this field at school level. The courses now place emphasis on the design as well as the making of objects. Girls tend to be reflective and take more care at this initial design stage. Boys tend to rush into the making process without adequate planning. The second factor is that women teachers have tended to prevail in the newly created Design and Technology departments (Paechter and Head, 1996a). These departments were formed from the amalgamation of male-dominated craft areas, notably woodwork and metalwork, with female-dominated home economics. This amalgamation has not always been easy, but the research suggests that the women have been more skilled in the team building and in getting others to go along with their perceptions of what the work should be like.

The products made by girls and boys differ, with the former looking at the human relevance and the latter at a 'technical fix'. One exercise I observed involved students aged 15 constructing a model of a house served by a low voltage electrical supply. The girls took great care in designing the house, making models of the furniture and painting the inside the rooms. They showed little interest in the use of electricity and contented themselves with a simple lighting circuit. The only science they learnt in this exercise came from those who wired the lights up in series so that if one light was switched off the whole house would be in darkness. The boys' houses were crude, just four bare walls. They made no effort to differentiate between the rooms. What excited them was building some intricate electrical system, with smoke alarms and burglar alarms being the most popular. Some of the work was most elaborate. One group used a pressure pad under the front door mat to set off the burglar alarm. Then they realized that the household cat might trigger it and adjusted the device so that a certain minimum weight was needed to activate it. Then they recognized a further problem, that everyone entering the house set off the alarm, so they now had to devise a time delaying device which would allow the owner of the house time to cancel the alarm before it went off. There was a clear gender division in their choice of where they concentrated their efforts.

Holyfield (1989) reports her efforts to persuade girls to study electronics. She found that if she used the components as the unit of analysis then the boys did better. If, however, the circuits were envisaged in terms of systems then the girls fared better. This difference clearly reflects the cognitive style difference between holistic and serial/analytical thinking. This example illustrates the point that the response to a subject is very dependent on the way the material is presented.

With Information Technology we have the curious situation of women being the main users, particularly with word-processing and the keeping of accounts, but with men dominating the academic study of computer sciences. When computers were first widely encountered in the early 1980s boys initially tended to see word-processors as glorified typewriters, fit for women working in offices. By the end of that decade the widespread use by boys of computer games meant that 80 per cent of home computers bought by parents were for their sons rather than their daughters. In school boys tend to move to the keyboard as of right and unless classes are carefully managed girls may find it difficult to gain much hands-on experience. As noted earlier in this chapter, this liking of boys for using computers can be utilized to help address achievement in literacy. To some extent the use of computer games has yielded ground to surfing the Internet, which boys see as a challenge to their technical skills. In such a rapidly developing field it is difficult to predict the future impact of information and communication technology on gender and education.

Physical Education

There is a major change in shifting attention from the core subjects of the National Curriculum to physical education, but for several reasons the latter subject is particularly pertinent to this book. It generates strong emotions among the boys, being very popular for many in providing opportunity for physical activity compared to the constraints of other school work. For others, the subject is dreaded, being for them a site of endless humiliation. Additionally, the combination of informality and being an all-male space gives it a unique quality.

I must admit to feeling some ambivalence about many male PE teachers. Seeing them, track suited, leaning against the wall outside the staff-room talking to a group of boys, one feels respect for a teacher who is able to maintain a dialogue with some of the more difficult boys in the school, accompanied with concern that he may be reinforcing their philistine, macho values by centring the conversation on football. Presumably the benefit comes if he is able to gain acceptance with the youth by being able to share their interests and then use the trust built up to enlarge their horizons and extend their interests. If he can carry out this complex process he can be uniquely valuable in the school. Otherwise he may simply reinforce the worst characteristics of the young men.

I think that my ambivalence is shared by many in the profession. In some of our research we found, for example, that female PE teachers were finding it difficult to equate femininity with the pursuit of athleticism (Paechter and Head, 1996b). Some of the accounts from male PE teachers about their education in the subject make horrific reading. Skelton (1993) describes life within a college specializing in PE and the initiation ceremonies the PE recruits had to endure in the early 1980s. They had to strip off all their clothes and were covered head to foot in black shoe polish. Then they were set tasks:

> I had to run down to a local Kentucky Fried Chicken take away (about 2 miles) and find out the price of chicken, chips and coleslaw. I was to be naked apart from a jock-strap. The other three had to do the following tasks respectively: fill a milk bottle full of sperm during the course of the evening; run around the athletics track tied by the genitals to another fresher (from a different group of four); 'visit' a pair of PE 'slags' in one of the women's halls to be 'seduced'.
>
> (1993: 294)

Given this initiation into homoerotic sadism, although the senior PE students would certainly have been vociferous in their expressions of homophobia, it is not surprising that any initial sensitivity is likely to be extinguished among these young men. Parker commented on his study in a comprehensive school:

> Physical education would appear to represent a key site for the manifestation of violent and aggressive behaviour; in constituting a portion of the wider sporting sphere, activities within physical education might be regarded as conducive to the arousal of aggression and violence as a result of their competitive capacity.
>
> (1996a: 145)

He observed that this expression of aggression not only occurred within the formal physical activities themselves but among the boys in the changing rooms. These usually involved:

> acrobatic displays of kicking manoeuvres reminiscent of those associated with the martial arts. ... once inside the changing rooms, and whilst teachers were preoccupied with ineligible participants, pupils were at liberty to capitalise on their close, and seemingly fascinating, semi-naked proximity.
>
> (1996a: 145)

Reading these accounts it easy to see why the less athletic or smaller boy might dread PE. In a football match he is likely to exposed to a series of verbal criticisms punctuated by occasional acts in which he experiences physical humiliation. Much depends on the way the teacher organizes the tasks. If, for example, each boy has to jump over the same hurdle, then for some it will be an easy feat while for others it sets an impossible demand. Better management might make it possible for each pupil to be given an appropriate task, something which provides a challenge but is within the competence of the individual.

Given the widespread interest among males in sports and its significance within the peer group culture, physical education offers a prime site for effective work with boys, albeit these opportunities are often not realized.

The Teacher's Task

One fundamental consideration is implicit throughout this chapter and can be best summarized in the words of David Ausubel:

> If I had to reduce all of educational psychology to just one principle, I would say this: The most important single factor influencing learning is what the learner already knows. Ascertain this and teach him accordingly.
>
> (Ausubel, 1968: iv)

My only caveat is that I think the principle extends more widely than Ausubel's words suggest. Certainly it applies to the formal knowledge, that which has been taught and possibly learnt in previous lessons. Much learning depends on certain prerequisite knowledge being in place and absence or inattention may thwart that condition. Supply teachers deserve respect for having to work with unfamiliar classes and deserve praise if they go beyond the child-minding function and promote effective learning.

Ausubel's principle becomes even more relevant in the light of research within the past two decades, revealing the constructivist nature of learning. Learners do not enter the classroom with empty minds but are likely to have prior beliefs about the lesson topic which may be incorrect and hinder learning. These concepts, based on a mix of their every day experience and folk wisdom, can be resistant to change. Again, the starting point for the teacher is to know what the pupils think about the topic prior to instruction.

Perhaps even more important is something which is probably beyond what Ausubel had in mind. Much of the argument in this chapter is not solely about the intellectual or cognitive but is concerned with feelings and values. The prevailing laddish, philistine ethos, which characterizes the male peer group, may be the biggest challenge to the teacher. They attach values to issues and subjects. In writing about the psychology of science Maslow suggested that the image of the scientist resembled that of the Hollywood cowboy, adding:

> look at the acting out and fantasy elements in the cowboy figure. ... The most obvious characteristics of the boy's dream of glory are there... He is fearless, he is strong, he is 'lone'. ... Apart from his horse he doesn't love anyone, or at least he doesn't express it. ... He is in every respect imaginable the far, polar opposite of the pansy type of homosexual in whose realm he includes all the arts, all of culture.
>
> (1966: 37)

Addressing these emotional prejudices of young men is likely to be more difficult than simply dealing with deficiencies in their academic knowledge. Too direct a challenge may prove threatening and stifle discussion. Somehow we have to reach out, start talking about issues in ways they understand, and quietly lead them to consider alternative perspectives, so that they can show empathy for others and be more at ease with themselves.

8   Schooling and Behaviour

The focus in this chapter is on behaviour, rather than academic achievement in schools and, in particular, how schools help shape behaviour. The plan is to start with a general description of schools as social institutions and then look in some detail as specific matters, such as bullying, sex education and pastoral work.

Schools Matter

This sub-heading may seem to be self-evident yet over the last two or three decades considerable attention has been given to factors external to schools which have been seen to limit what schools can achieve. The pioneering work of sociologists such as Douglas (1964) drew attention to the multiple deprivation some social groups experience and how this deprivation impacted on behaviour and work of individuals in schools. Willis (1977) made a slightly different point: that students may find themselves placed between two conflicting cultures, the essentially middle-class academic culture of the school and that of a working-class home. In this event, Willis argued, the students might ally themselves with their family roots and resist the efforts of teachers. In educational psychology both the earlier use of intelligence tests for selection, and the more recent use of Piaget's notion of stages in cognitive development, have caused us to see pupils as having fixed abilities which limit their performance. Given these beliefs, poor behaviour or work could be attributed to social and psychological factors beyond the competence of the school to address. I do not wish to deny the reality of these notions. Some children are cleverer or more co-operative than others, but what the students bring with them to school is only part of the picture. The way the school functions matters and, to some extent, can ameliorate or even overcome disadvantages.

Perhaps the key text in causing us to rethink our stance is that of Rutter et al. (1979), although it took some time for its significance to be widely appreciated. This book reports a study of ten comprehensive schools in the London area which revealed that on any measure, of academic success or of behaviour, some schools were better than others, despite having a similar intake. They identified the key to success being the effectiveness of the school as a social institution:

> schools which did better than average in terms of children's behaviour also tended to do better than average in terms of examination success. ... the differences between schools in outcomes were systematically related to their characteristics as social institutions.
>
> (1979: 178)

The general observations of Rutter are pertinent to the specific issues relating to boys. Mac an Ghaill made an extended study of the development of masculinity in one secondary school and reported how his research focus changed through his experience in that school:

> My initial focus over-emphasized gender reproduction, with particular reference to male students' future social, occupational and domestic destinies. ... I began to view schools as sites for the production of sex/gender subjectivities, where people conform, deviate, challenge, participate. ... the school microcultures of management, teachers and students are key infrastructural mechanisms through which masculinities and feminities are mediated and lived out.
>
> (1994: 2–4)

Connell points out that different boys will follow different paths to adopt different forms of masculinity:

> It is indeed important to recognise that different masculinities are being produced. ... These 'choices' are strongly structured by relations of power. In each of the cases mentioned, the differentiation of masculinities occurs in relation to the school curriculum which organises knowledge hierarchically, and sorts students into an academic hierarchy. By institutionalising academic failure via competitive grading and streaming, the school forces differentiation on the boys. ... The reaction of the 'failed' is likely to be a claim to other sources of power, even other definitions of masculinity. Sporting success, physical aggression, sexual conquest may do.
>
> (1989: 295)

The current problem in relation to academic achievement is that in schools the 'other sources of power' may dominate within the peer group. Sport, aggression and sex may become the defining characteristics of the dominant boys and the academically successful are dismissed as being 'swots' or 'boffins'. The task for the school is to provide opportunities for boys of all abilities to gain their sense of masculinity through socially acceptable ways.

What makes a successful school is difficult to summarize, but some key characteristics are having a clear policy and expectations coming from the senior staff, ensuring that teachers, parents and pupils are aware of these policies, so that they can work together within a common framework towards common goals. If we have to select one single variable as having causal significance I think it must be the quality of the headteacher.

When schools started to draw up policy statements on matters such as equity or bullying I was initially slightly sceptical, fearing that having generated the rhetoric teachers may fail to go further and look at the realities. That danger is real, but it has become recognized that drawing up policies serves both to draw attention to problems and to provide a systematic framework in which individual actions can be taken. The starting point for addressing the problems with boys is to make a commitment to take action and involves parents and students in seeing this commitment being realized. Mechanisms have to be in place to ensure these outcomes, and, in turn, the mechanisms have to be reviewed at intervals to ensure that they are working. A school may claim that it provides career guidance, a tutoring system and pastoral care, but their effectiveness remains to be demonstrated. Looking at some specific initiatives should illustrate this point.

Bullying

Bullying is by no means a new problem, as books such as *Tom Brown's Schooldays* show, but recently there has been an increased awareness of it. Perhaps in the past it was too commonly believed that children were essentially good and could be left to sort out their own relationships with their peers. Unfortunately, there is abundant evidence that even young children compete, argue, fight and bully unless constrained by adults. The extent of the problem is demonstrated by the appeals to agencies such as Childline, where it has become the most frequent reason for calling.

Estimates of the extent of bullying vary. Ahmad and Smith (1994) in one study found about half of the middle and secondary pupils reported being bullied at some time and 6–8 per cent reported that it happened to them at least every week. Throughout the system more boys were bullied than girls and the bullies were also more often boys. Less than 2 per cent of the boys reported that they were bullied by girls acting on their own but in middle schools the girls were more commonly bullied by boys than their own sex and even in secondary school 28 per cent of the bullying of girls was carried out by boys. There are gender differences in forms of bullying, with boys carrying out more physical acts, punching, tripping or taking property away, while girls use verbal criticism and sarcasm more.

There can be no doubt about the damage caused by bullying. The victims are likely to suffer from depression to the extent of attempting suicide. Their problem is that they feel so helpless. They are likely to be outnumbered by the bigger or stronger bullies so physical retaliation is unwise. They have been selected as victims for reasons beyond their control, usually for being seen as 'different', sometimes because of ethnicity, more commonly nowadays because they are quieter, more scholarly boys who are labelled as 'poofs', and as such merit beating. Mahony pointed out that 'When a boy gets "pushed around" it is not, I would suggest, in virtue of being a boy, but because he is not the right sort of boy' (1989: 162). For the bullies the experience tends to lead to the adoption of habits of violence leading on to criminality (Cullingford and Morrison, 1995).

Mynard and Joseph (1997) report a study made of 179 pupils, aged between eight and 13, in which they found 11 per cent could be classed as bullies, 20 per cent as victims and 18 per cent were both victims and bullies. They found that the latter two groups typically had different personality characteristics, based on psychometric testing. Those who were solely victims tended to be introverted. Possibly they were naturally loners and could be picked off as victims as they lacked a network of supportive friends. Those who were both victims and bullies show greater disturbance, being high on both the neuroticism and psychoticism scales. Children in this latter group seem to act out their feelings of inferiority through being bullied by bullying others. Mynard and Joseph sum up this finding:

> What seems to set bully/victims apart most of all is their low level of social acceptance. ... it is known that children may behave aggressively after having seen a model act aggressively. ... those who are most strongly influenced by model effects are those who do not have a natural status among their peers and would like to assert themselves.
>
> (1997: 54)

Despite these findings the extent of bullying is determined as much by the ethos of the school as by the behaviour of individuals. In recent decades our understanding has changed from simply seeing bullies as suffering from some character defect, to having the idea that the habit is spread like a contagious disease, so that the bullied become bullies in turn, to the recognition of the importance of the school ethos. Cullingford and Morrison sum up their research findings: 'The problem is not a matter of clearly isolated incidents and individuals. It is pervasive in the social life of the school, and therefore all children are affected by it in one form or another' (1995: 547). There is widespread evidence that the biggest fear of primary school boys about the transfer to secondary school is that they are going to be very vulnerable in the new situation.

Given this evidence it is clearly vital for a school to establish an anti-bullying policy and, more importantly, put in place mechanisms to see that it is enforced. Parents should be told of this initiative and asked to cooperate by reporting problems their children experience. The worrying finding I encounter is that in many schools teachers admit that they have no idea of what bullying may be going on and simply hope that the existence of an official policy statement will suffice. Obviously the ethic of not being a sneak is likely to prevail among the students, but it is possible to gain generalized reports from the pupils. If pupils are asked to write anonymously about the extent of bullying and, crucially, the most common location and timing, teachers should gain enough information to be able to minimize the problem. The final task is to use every opportunity within the school to propagate the message that bullying is completely unacceptable and that all should work together to prevent it.

There is a large literature advising on bullying. Some deal with the broad picture, e.g. Tattum and Herbert (1993), which includes dealing with school management policies, using the curriculum, handling primary to secondary transition and the role of Local Education Authorities. Other texts, e.g. Donellan (1998), provide specific suggestions for use in school and the workplace.

Sex Education

Despite the increased attention paid to sex education in recent times, particularly because of the fears relating to HIV/AIDS, it is evident that it is not achieving its aims. One measure is the pregnancy rate of girls under 16, where Britain has one of the highest figures in Europe, with 7,300 cases in 1993 of which 3,800 had an abortion. The government *Health of the Nation* aim is to reduce that figure to 4,800 by the year 2000, but there has been no sign of this reduction taking place. There is ample evidence that despite the fact that young men are fully aware about the use of condoms to ensure safe sex they still prefer not to use them. The most comprehensive study of sexual behaviour in Britain is that of Wellings et al. (1994) who surveyed a population of 20,000. They found that although about 60 per cent of the sexually active men and 40 per cent of the active women aged between 16 and 24 used condoms, a third of the men and half of the women who were not in a stable relationship still failed to use them. A similar picture has been widely reported, e.g. by Murphy et al. (1998) and Gilbert and Gilbert (1998). Clearly the messages about safe sex practices are not being heard. Many young men dislike the use of condoms, arguing it interferes with their pleasure and challenges their macho sense of being 'chancers'.

The main problem is that there are several possible agendas relating to sex education and the teachers often have an agenda which is totally different from that of young men.

Teachers still tend to employ a scientific, objective approach to the subject. There are some merits in this stance, as we must provide an adequate factual base for discussion and understanding of the issues that take place. The problem is that the process often does not go beyond the mechanics of sexual behaviour. One consequence is that there is a degree of repetition, as the boys receive sex education at various stages in their schooling. They claim the work is boring as they know it all already. In part such a claim may be bravado to gain peer group approval but there is probably some reality to it as well. They also complain that the teacher makes no reference to the idea that sexual activity might be enjoyable. It is described in terms of it being a necessary task – like cleaning the kitchen. Nor is there any reference to the emotions associated with sex, notably falling in love. For the youngsters sex generates a mix of emotions, fear, excitement, curiosity and doubt, yet the issue is too often discussed without any of these emotional concerns being recognized.

The prime concern for the boys, for reasons that were discussed in Chapter 4, is with their own performance. This anxiety may be revealed by joking, for example a boy claiming that a condom is too small to fit him, in asking questions about different positions and other ways to heighten sexual satisfaction, or asking for reassurance that 'size does not matter'. If the education is to be effective these concerns have to be addressed at some stage. If, however, we do not listen to the young men but give a didactic lesson on our agenda then the unsatisfactory outcome is scarcely surprising.

Because of the sensitivity required to discuss these concerns it may be better to conduct at least part of a sex education programme within single-sex groups. The presence of girls both promotes macho boasting and embarrassment, which can lead to disruptive behaviour, such as throwing contraceptive devices around the room. An experienced worker in this field, Davidson, writes:

> the focus of the work described here is a single-sex setting. This is so for two reasons. Firstly, we haven't traditionally thought very clearly or positively about young men's sex education needs. Single-sex work gives us the opportunity to find out more about the part sex and relationships play in their lives. Secondly, it allows young men the space to break free of the stereotypical attitudes and behaviour which inevitably arises in mixed groups.
>
> (1997: 27)

There is evidence of sex differences in the response of adolescents to sex education. Measor et al. observed a calm, purposeful lesson with a group of girls and contrasted that with a mixed group in the same school: 'the room seemed to be overflowing with people, noise, chaos and disruption, pushing and shoving. Bags were thrown and so were half-serious punches; chairs squeaked and scraped, boys squirmed and desks rattled' (1996: 278). They went on to add 'boys objected more strongly and openly than girls to the sex education material'.

My own observation of classes in secondary school reveals that boys are more embarrassed and squeamish. The former feeling is shown most with respect to talk about male anatomy and functioning and the latter in respect to the female anatomy and matters such as menstruation. Overall, the boys are not at ease with their own bodies, and the extent of their disruption indicates the extent of anxiety these lessons unearth.

There is a third agenda in addition to those described to date. We tend to separate sex education from other work, sometimes to the extent of bringing in outsiders to undertake the lesson. What is missing, then, is the location of sexual interests and activity within the wider social setting. Adolescents may know all about the mechanics of conceiving a child but have no appreciation of what is involved in child care. A comprehensive programme would deal with such matters and also the emotional responses we have to sex.

For those seeking more detailed ideas about possible lessons Davidson (1997) provides a number of ideas for working with young men, covering the obvious topics of contraception and disease, but also raising discussions on the nature of sexuality and the common myths about men. Salisbury and Jackson (1996) provide lesson plans for a wide range of topics, including a discussion on what makes someone attractive, masturbation, sexual myths and bisexuality. Both sources address the more biological aspects as well, for example asking the boys to name the parts shown on drawings of male and female genitalia. Both try to reduce embarrassment by looking at the language, vernacular and medical, used in relation to sex, and in so doing indicating that it is legitimate to use these words within these lessons.

Discussion of homosexuality remains a problem. Davidson notes:

> Talking about homosexuality brings up young men's defensive attitudes more readily than anything else. The fear and anxiety in the room is almost tangible. I believe that many young men's fear of gay men is based on a deep-rooted fear of other men and a fragile sense of what 'being a man' is all about. The subject of homosexuality brings to the surface what is there all the time.
>
> (1997: 58–9)

I have found that the only tactic which allows a reasoned discussion on homosexuality is to start by suggesting that those who have a firm sense of their own preferences and identity are not threatened by a calm, reasoned discussion. The emotions shown by those who become aggressive or disruptive reveal uncertainties and anxiety about their own sexuality. Having established this point, which echoes the findings discussed earlier in studies of the authoritarian personality, it becomes difficult for any boy to do other than calmly listen and talk about the subject.

Forrest et al. (1997) have produced for AVERT (the Aids Education and Research Trust) a useful book on talking about homosexuality in secondary schools. It offers advice on a wide range of issues, from involving parents and managing lessons, to suggestions for lesson content. It provides a uniquely valuable resource for teachers.

Citizenship and Moral Education

As a consequence of the introduction of 'league tables' of school academic successes at GCSE and earlier Key Stages in the National Curriculum, schools have tended to increasingly direct their efforts to performance in these subjects to the neglect of social, personal and health education. An awareness of this deficiency has been growing and the publication of the Crick Report in 1998 relating to citizenship has drawn further attention to the situation. Discussion is currently taking place as to whether education in citizenship should be a mandatory element in the school curriculum.

The underlying influences have been many. One concern is with crime. There has been an enormous increase in crime prevention measures in recent years, with surveillance cameras installed in many car parks, railway stations and shopping centres, with security staff on duty at city buildings ranging from schools to pubs and shops, while cars are now fitted with a host of anti-theft devices and many homes have burglar alarms. Despite all these measures crime figures have tended to increase. Given that situation we face three possible scenarios: crime rates may be allowed to increase, more and more security measures are put into effect even though they may be seen as inconvenient and an invasion of privacy, or somehow we are able to persuade more people in our society to stay within the law themselves and influence others to do likewise.

In part it is a matter of gaining youths' allegiance and respect for authority. The increased lack of respect on the part of young people for authority figures, parents, teachers and the police, has already been described in this book (see Chapter 6). If authority cannot be imposed by external agents then the possibility of helping young people to act more responsibly of their own volition must be explored as the most acceptable way forward. If a programme of education for citizenship is established then it has ramifications for pastoral work with boys and young men, if only because they are the main offenders in society.

We have seen with respect to sex education and also the issue of drug use that many educational programmes have not been very successful in influencing the behaviour of young people. It is a different form of education from that which most commonly goes on in schools. In most areas success can be measured through what is written in tests and examinations. However, in any form of moral education it is only too easy for the students to express one set of sentiments on paper and then behave according to totally different precepts when outside school, particularly if they are within a peer group. The more we try to extract statements which we consider desirable from students the greater the danger that we are encouraging increasing hypocrisy in which rhetoric and reality are far apart.

This problem is common to much within social and personal education and points to the need to develop a sophisticated analysis of pedagogic practices and student outcomes. There are places in the literature where this process is taking place. For example, Zigler (1998) develops a taxonomy for moral education, using two variables to create four domains. The first variable is external–internal, reminding us that the problems are not only among us, i.e. in society, but are also within us, invoking such qualities as moral character. The second variable is direct–indirect, referring to the ways the educational messages are conveyed.

With the direct–external domain we are describing a didactic approach in which students are helped to understand moral issues in general and the norms of the school in particular. These precepts can then be put into practice by setting behavioural targets for working within the school.

The indirect–external domain is reflected in the overall moral climate and culture of the school. Zigler warns us 'if the school culture is not consciously addressed by school faculty and administration, the peer group – and media – will fill the vacuum' (1998: 29). The desirable school culture is one which reflects a respect for people and socially responsible behaviour.

The direct–internal domain is concerned to promote mature autonomous behaviour, arguing that 'the mature individual finds ethical conduct *intrinsically* rewarding, unlike less mature individuals who may conform to avoid punishment or social condemnation' (1998: 29). To facilitate the development of this behaviour schools should provide what he calls 'a moment of silence', in other words opportunities to reflect and escape for a while from the pressure to respond to external demands and other people. Interestingly, schools for emotionally disturbed children have long had a practice of setting aside a place where a child can go for a while when stressed and be left alone until feeling able to cope with the teacher and peers.

The final domain, the indirect–internal area, invokes the notion of emotional literacy (Goleman, 1996), in which individuals develop the capacity to recognize and modify their own emotions and exercise empathy in recognizing the emotions of others. Essentially, the individual has to learn to monitor the signs of emotional stress and take constructive measures to reduce or usefully channel these feelings.

Zigler argues that all four domains are needed in moral education and any school programme should pay attention to all of them. I am not seeking to advance this particular taxonomy to the exclusion of others, but have quoted it to demonstrate what personal and social education, such as in dealing with citizenship, involves.

Boyswork

All the initiatives described hitherto in this chapter can be seen as part of a mainstream school curriculum, equally applicable to boys and girls. In this section I want to review the work which has been developed specifically for boys and the potential for further progress in this field.

Part of the feminist movement in the 1960s was the creation of various groups and organizations to help women. Some of these were very specific in their purpose, for example in providing support for those who suffered from abusive partners, while other groups were more general, providing a social and supportive network for women. Eventually these developments extended into many secondary schools. Sometimes the intention was to tackle specific problems, for example, in order to counteract the tendency of boys to dominate the hands-on work with computers, computer clubs for girls would be set up to operate during the lunch break. Other sessions might be devoted to assertiveness training, to help girls hold their own in dealing with boys, whether in resisting sexual harassment or in the general give-and-take of school life.

There was some reaction from boys that they were being left out; the needs of girls were being met, but not the needs of boys. One difficulty at this stage was that little thought had been given to what it was that boys might need. Much of the initial work for boys was designed by women to force boys address their sexist behaviour (e.g. Whyld, 1986). Exercises were developed to demonstrate the common use of sexist language in talking about girls and how boys exerted social pressure and dominance in their dealings with girls.

Work of this kind was justified as it helped develop a social ethos in a school in which racist and sexist behaviour was minimized. It had, however, two weaknesses. It tended to alienate boys, who felt themselves to be victimized by receiving nothing but blame for what they did (Kenway, 1995). There seemed to be no benefit from such work for the boys. Second, it was addressing symptoms of male behaviour and not the causes. It is one of my main themes in this book that males are not inherently bad, but that anti-social behaviour arises from certain pressures to which young men are subjected, and the starting point for any reform is to understand the situation they find themselves in. For such work to succeed it must be based on a recognition of the fears, beliefs and values of these young men, rather than subjecting them to an agenda drawn up by others. Any scheme of boyswork, therefore, involves listening to boys. It requires an ethos in which they can talk relatively freely about sensitive areas, such as sexuality, health, bullying and relationships, rather than operate within the usual macho discourse. The boys need to emerge from the experience with the recognition that they have gained something valuable from it.

It has only been since about the mid-1990s that work within this genre has been developed and the literature is still small. I will describe three texts to illustrate the current range of material currently available.

Francis edited a booklet for the Shropshire Education Authority with the declared aim to 'enable boys to think about themselves and their role, and be more confident about how they might develop'. He lists the common criticisms of young men but points out that 'Boys are more likely to commit assault than girls, but they are also more likely to be the victims. ... Men may be at the top of the heap, but they are not sitting there serenely; many are confused and under pressure' (1994: 5).

The booklet then contains a number of exercises which can be carried in schools, preferably, he argues, with male teachers. There are four talking assignments, about issues such as reviewing what we know about gender differences and the current state of gender relations in our society. Eight possible reading assignments cover such topics as an analysis of gender in the labour market, reports by various men of the pressures they experience and the role of fathers. Finally, there are seven research assignments which involve the students eliciting from men and women, boys and girls, their views on the issues which have already been encountered in the talking and reading units.

It is not suggested that every school could use every assignment but a bank of ideas is provided. This text has two clear merits, it is written by a serving teacher and hence is realistic, and it is written with great sensitivity. The main limitation is that the range of topics covered is quite narrow and certain key areas such as health and sexual behaviour are not included.

The second source, that of Lloyd (1997), is different in that it describes initiatives outside school, essentially in youth work. It contains accounts of twelve such initiatives: including work in a drop-in clinic dealing with issues such as safe sex and testicular cancer; discussion of masculinity with young men in response to talk within an all-male dance class; working with victims of bullying in local schools; working with ethnic minorities and with those experiencing learning disabilities. In general, the young men described here are older than those in secondary school and that fact, combined with the more informal atmosphere of the youth settings, allowed a freer choice of topics. Nevertheless, it ought to be possible to adapt many of these ideas for work within school.

By far the most comprehensive collection of ideas for boyswork in school is found in Salisbury and Jackson (1996). Both the authors had over twenty years experience of secondary school teaching by the time they wrote this book. They have chapters on such matters as boys' sexualities, sexual harassment, bullying and violence, the ideal manly body, language as a weapon, sport, fathers and sons. Each chapter starts with a review of current evidence and beliefs about the topic and then contains a number suggested activities which could be undertaken in school. Fairly detailed instructions are provided for carrying out each activity, with aims specified, a list of materials needed for the lesson and plan of how the session might be organized. This collection is by far the most ambitious initiative to date in the field of boyswork and hence represents the state of the art. One criticism of the book is that it might be too comprehensive and a bit repetitive, so that with over 300 pages it is not easy for a teacher to quickly search for and identify something required for a specific purpose.

With all these lists of proposed activities teachers will need to select and adapt according to what they know about the class. One activity suggested in the Salisbury and Jackson chapter on the body starts with boys being asked to draw an ideal male body. We can wonder how an inexperienced teacher might cope with the disruption as the boys allow their phallic imagination free rein. An experienced teacher would recognize this potential for unrest and might forestall it by telling the boys that a joking attitude reveals immaturity or personal disquiet about one's own body.

Although all these schemes have been tried out to some extent, it is true that boyswork is still too new for there to be feedback from a wide variety of schools about a wide range of materials. Only when that has been achieved will there be an agreed corpus of material available for teachers. Scope remains for the development, trialling, revision and dissemination of materials in this field. As noted earlier, personal and social education has been squeezed to a minimum in many secondary schools as they are concerned to gain academic success in the main curriculum subjects. There are signs of pastoral work being more valued again and a collection of material for use with boys might form part of the new offerings.

The Good-Enough School: A Checklist

Psychologists working in counselling and therapy are often reluctant to use labels, such a 'good father' or a 'good husband', for sound reasons. The terms might suggest that there exists some ideal to which all should conform, and we might fail to acknowledge both the diversity and imperfections found among people. For this reason the practice has developed of talking about the 'good-enough father', for instance. This label is seen to recognize that the person has his own individual mix of good and less good qualities, but overall he is able to act satisfactorily as a father. I want to take a parallel approach to schools. No school will be perfect, and some bullying and so forth might occur. Schools also differ, so that what is tolerated within one school may not be in another. Within broad limits these differences do not matter provided the school itself is consistent. Given these limitations the concept of a good-enough school is the appropriate one for setting up criteria to monitor schools. No claim is being made that the following list of criteria is completely comprehensive, and different schools will choose to focus on some items more than others, but the list should serve as an indication of the quality of provision.

1   Has the school produced policy statements on matters such as equity and bullying? Are these comprehensive, e.g. is reference made to the bullying of gay students? Although nearly all schools have a statement on bullying in place, fewer than 10 per cent mention homophobia, an omission which can be interpreted as giving tacit permission to bully these students.

2   Are policies and practices fully discussed among staff, and with pupils and parents? This exchange should be two-way, so that all are clearly informed what is school policy, but additionally feedback is needed from pupils and parents about what reality the pupils experience. For

example, can teachers confidently claim that they know the extent and location of bullying and are taking steps to meet the specific areas of concern? The effectiveness of school policies largely depends on all the various interest groups working together to carry out these policies.

3   Is comprehensive vocational guidance offered? In many schools the career teacher and career room have gone and outside agencies are brought in to help. These professionals can introduce some useful ideas, for example asking students to draw up action plans for them to find out about careers and make the appropriate academic choices. Relying on these external agencies alone is not satisfactory as their staff do not know the individual students. Those who know the youngsters well, their personal qualities and their academic record, are better placed to cover some aspects of guidance.

4   Are health education and sex education courses responsive to the needs and concerns of the boys? For example, are they advised about testicular cancer? Is there some mechanism by which the pupils can raise issues without suffering from embarrassment? It is possible, for example, to ask the members of a class to write questions on a piece of paper without having to give their name. The list of questions provides an agenda for part of this work.

5   Within a coeducational school is there any provision for boys and girls to meet separately with staff in order to raise matters which concern many within the group but which they do not want to discuss in front of those of the other sex?

6   Is there an effective mechanism for individual boys to seek advice from staff without having to go through a complicated or embarrassing procedure? Many tutorial groups, or their equivalent, are conducted with one staff member working with a small group of students. This arrangement works well most of the time but may not be adequate in itself. One way out is to make an individual tutorial mandatory once a term. If the arrangement is not mandatory then boys who need help may not seek it, partly from the widespread reluctance of males to ask for assistance, and specifically within a school they do not want to be identified by their peers as needing help. With the mandatory system all boys have to attend such a meeting but no one else knows what is discussed, whether it is merely a routine review of progress or a consideration of some deeper personal problem.

7   Does the school provide a reasonable range of facilities for its students? I have in mind here not the provision of specialist rooms for academic work, although these are vitally important, but such things as a homework club or room. We know that boys tend to give less attention to this work than girls, partly because they are easily distracted when at home. The provision of a quiet space where students can go to work if they wish to helps them establish better work habits, and, interestingly,

the provision generally proves to be well-used. If some social space is also available then many students might spend time in the evening moving between the homework area and the social provision. This must be a better alternative for them than hanging around the street corners.

9 Boys at the Margins

In this chapter consideration is given to boys who might be considered to be on the margins of normality, either because of their behaviour, such as school refusal or violence, or such psychological dispositions as dyslexia or autism. Many such boys are handled outside the conventional school and family provision and as such are beyond the purview of this book. Others may show less extreme characteristics and might be encountered within mainstream schooling. So, although no detailed consideration of professional practice is given here, a brief overview is provided as it might enhance understanding of how young men operate.

Ideally I would like to structure this chapter thematically, with like behaviours or characteristics clustered together. However, the definitions are often so vague that such ordering might suggest a greater clarity than exists in reality. I have decided, therefore, simply to provide an alphabetical listing of the six commonest conditions.

Many of the categories, including dyslexia, autism and those described as meaning a child has Special Needs, are much more common among boys than girls, with, in most cases, boys making up about 80 per cent of the particular population. This consistency in ratio between the sexes might imply a genetic causation, but the actual figures have been challenged. It has been argued that girls suffering from these conditions are more likely to be left within mainstream schools as they are less disruptive than their male counterparts. If this suggestion is valid then many girls who might benefit from special attention are being left within schools to cope on their own.

Attention Deficit Hyperactivity Disorder (ADHD)

This condition has gained a lot of attention in recent years, with suggestions that it affects about 3–5 per cent of the population, mainly boys. The concept of attention deficit has a long history, and refers to the characteristics of a pupil who is reasonably intelligent but whose academic work is of an erratic standard. When the student concentrates on the task the work is satisfactory but too frequently inattention brings about confusion.

Sometimes the pupil has not listened to the initial instructions, and either seems bewildered when asked to start the task, or plunges in with no clear sense of how to proceed. On other occasions such children may start satisfactorily but then become distracted and wander off to do something quite different.

More recently the concept of hyperactivity has been added on to complement the description of attention deficit. The hyperactive child tends to be restless, enjoying the stimulus of new activities, and quickly becoming bored with routine and breaking off from one activity to seek new stimulus. This cluster of characteristics becomes manifest quite early in school years, usually well before adolescence. All sufferers are likely to achieve well below what appears to be their academic potential. More extreme cases experience greater handicaps, for example no one is safe driving a car unless they have the capacity to concentrate on that task and ignore the distractions which might be seen from out of the window.

Various causal factors have been postulated for ADHD, but any explanation has to account for the apparent increase in hyperactivity in recent years. One suggestion is that of changes in diet, with some food additives, notably tartrazine, generating allergic reactions. Many food manufacturers have substituted natural colourings, such as carotene as a replacement. Another idea is that young people are exposed to too stimulating an environment, spending leisure time visiting theme parks and being with the television or computer much of the time at home. The argument is that children become conditioned to this constant exposure to thrills and excitement and are not happy without it. Another possibility is that the incidence of ADHD has not increased but we have simply become more aware of it.

Not only is the condition more common among boys but it can be seen as an extension of normal male behaviour. McGuiness (1985) found even among 'normal' children gender differences in their play. The boys she observed averaged four and a half activities within a 20-minute period while the girls averaged two and a half. Boys interrupted what they were doing three times more often than the girls. McGuiness indicated that girls are likely to work about twice as long on an activity started by a teacher than the boys. This finding can be interpreted as a social difference, with the girls relating more closely to adults while boys assert their autonomy.

It remains uncertain how effective we can be in helping children combat ADHD. The common practice is to slow them down and get them to check their understanding of the task and to plan their work before actually starting it, hoping that this training will help them develop good work habits. Much depends on how deep-rooted the condition might be and whether there is a biochemical causal element.

Autism

Our immediate problem is that this term is used loosely, to describe at least three conditions: the classical autism of a severe mental handicap manifested in children, Asperger's Syndrome which can be seen as a variant of the main condition and mild autistic tendencies which are quite widespread among the population. I will treat the three in that sequence.

The classical form of autism was first described in the early 1940s and the central characteristic is that the child seems to have a 'person blindness', so that he or she fails to recognize the needs of other people. In the home any child has access to objects, ranging from a chair to a television set, which are there to be used. An autistic child attributes the same status to other members of the family, they are there to be used at the convenience of the child. Typical symptoms are lack of interest in other people and the avoidance of eye contact, and these symptoms will be manifest in early childhood, so autism can usually be diagnosed before the age of 5. The child will not respect the privacy or possessions of others and may enter a sibling's room, interrupt whatever they are doing and walk away with the sibling's toys. Even among the less severe cases the children have no sense of what is socially appropriate and may disturb a lunch party by talking about their own sexual interests or someone's medical problems. Although they often ignore others they may on occasion seek the reassurance of being cuddled, but again lack social intelligence by asking a complete stranger for this service.

Severe autism is fortunately rare, affecting less than 1 per 1,000 children. It is far more common among boys which might be partly explained by the finding that in some cases it is associated with a fragile X-chromosome syndrome (Hagerman and Sobesky, 1989). Sometimes autism has been described a juvenile form of schizophrenia, which itself tends to become manifest in adolescence or early adulthood. There are some resemblances, but schizophrenics often display additional characteristics, various irrational behaviours, such as hearing voices, perhaps having paranoid illusions about others.

One former myth about the condition is that it results from the experience of childhood neglect or abuse. In fact, most autistic children come from loving and supportive families.

Asperger's Syndrome describes young people who have many autistic characteristics but also are highly intelligent or gifted. I have on file a description of a 16-year-old autistic boy who had his collection of architectural drawings published, and an account of a 35-year-old concert pianist who is incapable of looking after himself. Whereas the classical case of autism nearly always means that the child has to be removed from mainstream schooling with the Asperger's Syndrome boy we can help him use his intelligence to control his behaviour. Barber (1996) describes a programme in which a 15-year-old boy was presented with a list of undesirable behaviours, such as shouting or running around the classroom, and had to identify those which he most commonly did. In this way he built up a picture of his strengths and weaknesses and used this to monitor and seek to improve his behaviour. In more technical language, a form of cognitive therapy was employed to enhance his ego strength. This tactic allowed him to be integrated into a mainstream school.

Just as we can see a continuum between full-blown ADHD and typical behaviour of many boys, so it is possible to identify mild autistic qualities among many boys. The inability to confront and talk about emotions is probably the most common characteristic, and this point was discussed more fully in Chapter 5. A lack of social intelligence is another common feature among young males. Perhaps the most obvious point is that many boys opt to spend their leisure times in pursuits such as fishing, where they sit for hours in silence on a wet river bank, or playing with their computers. Concern has been expressed in the literature about boys who seemed to use the computer as a substitute for any social contact with others. Presumably what we are witnessing with these instances of mild autistic tendencies is not a biological condition, such as the fragile X-chromosome, but the product of social rearing in which boys are encouraged to pursue autonomy and not express their feelings.

Depression and Suicide

There are some curious gender differences in this area. More young women than men report depression and more carry out some physical act of self-harm, such as cutting their wrists, but far more young men actually commit suicide.

The most likely explanation for this pattern of behaviour is that young men tend to believe that they must manage their own life whereas young woman will be more ready to admit to having problems and seek help from others. If this is the case we may not really know the incidence of depression among young men. It is also possible than many acts of self-mutilation by females are a cry for help rather than a serious suicide bid. If the males believe that they cannot ask for help then they can see no alternative to suicide itself.

Whatever the explanation we are left with the fact that on average five men under the age of 35 commit suicide every day in this country. A proportion, between one fifth and quarter, have some history of mental disorder or stress , so they are recognizable as being at some risk. However, with the majority the suicide comes as a complete shock to family and friends, as the young men seemed to have everything to live for. The causal factors include unemployment, the break up of a close relationship with someone and excessive dependence on alcohol or drugs. Although these factors are clearly depressing we are dealing here with people who might be seen to have the capacity to cope. There seem to be no reasons to doubt that they can find another job or another girlfriend. The crucial factor for suicide seems to be the absence of a support system to help the person cope with the customary failures which we are all likely to experience. If these young men could face talking to someone, admitting their temporary incapacity to cope, then in many cases we might assume that they would recover their psychic equilibrium.

Dyslexia

Dyslexia is yet another condition found more commonly among boys. It is diagnosed in about four times as many boys as girls but it may be present in less extreme forms among many more boys and be a contributory factor for their poor literacy skills. The more extreme form, in which academic progress is markedly retarded, is recognized in between 2 and 4 per cent of the total population. About a further 6 per cent are believed to suffer to a lesser, but still significant, degree. The common symptoms are in spelling, in placing letters in an incorrect sequence, or in laterally inverting single letters while writing. It used to be believed that dyslexia was simply a disorder in perception, and a few books still describe it as such. There are several reasons to doubt this view. Many dyslexic boys are quite good at some spatial and perceptual tasks, showing good ability in drawing and in ball games. We now believe that the problem comes with the cognitive processing within the mind. Humans process incoming information through a series of stages. Information from the perceptual apparatus, in this case the eyes, initially is handled in the active part of the mind, using the short-term memory. If the information is deemed worthy of interest, and the mind has to be selective to avoid cognitive overload, then it has to be inserted into the cognitive structure of the long-term memory. We might use the analogy of placing a paper somewhere in a filing cabinet. Somewhere along the line something goes wrong with a dyslexic, the message has either not been copied properly or has been placed in the wrong file.

Why should this happen more with boys than girls? It may be because boys are more hasty and careless and an initial mistake is difficult to eradicate. Another explanation is that brains in males tend to be more compartmentalized and possibly this fact means that parts of the brain do not work so well together in handling information input.

Dyslexic boys do not suffer from impaired intelligence and improvement can be brought about by giving them special exercises. Typically they may be shown a diagram of a set of objects arranged along a shelf. They might be asked to copy the diagram and then draw another copy from memory. Such an exercise focuses attention on the sequence and orientation of the objects.

Statementing and Special Needs

Following the Warnock Report (DES, 1978) a new Education Act (DES, 1981) attempted to update the provision for children experiencing undue difficulty in mainstream schooling by replacing the system requiring precise diagnosis of a disability with the general notion of special educational needs (SEN). Overall about 20 per cent of the school population might have some need, but through the appointment of Specialist Needs Co-ordinators (SENCOs) in schools it was assumed that the vast majority of these children could be accommodated within these schools. For the minority who experienced more severe difficulties, about 2 per cent of the total school population, a process of Statementing would be initiated by the school and carried out by educational psychologists. Depending upon local arrangements a child identified in this way might be sent to a specialist SEN school or, if the mainstream school had adequate provision, could continue within the previous school, but receive additional help.

Initially this procedure was hailed as a major advance in provision, but since the change in funding and financing schools following the 1988 Education Reform Act a new factor has emerged. Schools are having to compete for pupils and hence funds, and poorly performing students will tend to reduce the overall score for academic success of the school. Having the less able pupils identified by Statementing can help in school in either one of two ways. If the pupils are removed and are sent to an SEN establishment the school has some of its academically weaker students removed so the average performance will be seen to increase. Even if these students are retained, the school gains extra funding and is able in quoting tables of academic achievement to point out that these pupils cannot really be included in the statistics for GCSE and allied examinations. Williams and Maloney sum up the situation:

> there is no doubt it led to schools examining more closely all aspects of resourcing and of being more likely to demand special resources for activities seen by them as outside the ordinary. The most obvious effect has been the rapid increase in the number of children with Statements in mainstream schools since 1990. ... it is likely that the rise in Statement numbers comes directly from groups of children, for whom schools would have previously made provision without Statements.
>
> (1998: 16)

There are three categories of Special Needs and boys are a large majority in all three. In the case of those categorized as having Severe Learning Difficulties the greater male vulnerability to disorders such as autism and chromosomal damage, e.g. Down's syndrome has an effect. The second category of Emotional and Behavioural Difficulties includes neurotic behaviour, where boys are not in a majority, but also anti-social behaviour, where the boys' more disruptive and violent behaviour causes them to be singled out. The third group, identified as experiencing Moderate Learning Difficulties, suffer most commonly from limited literacy skills, which impacts on their academic performance across the curriculum. Again the boys make up 75–80 per cent of this population. These pupils may do quite well in subjects which are less dependent on literacy, e.g. mathematics. Their poor command of the subtleties of language may account for the common report that these pupils can answer the factual (What?) questions but scarcely understand if asked about the (Why?) questions about causes or why they answered as they did.

What emerges from this section is the existence of a considerable proportion of children, varying between 2 per cent and 20 per cent according to the criteria employed, who are an educational underclass, and are labelled as such. The vast majority in this group are boys. In the past they could find unskilled work, and in some circumstances well-paid work, for example in mining. There is little provision for them today.

Truancy, Exclusion and Crime

I am using the word 'truancy' to cover a range of effects which stop pupils attending school. Some of them suffer from a school phobia in which some neurotic or irrational fear causes their behaviour. Other school refusers may have perfectly rational fears, for example, the knowledge that they are likely to be bullied if they do go to school. One truanting boy, in a school where I taught, eventually admitted that the cause of his behaviour was that he was disturbed by the fluorescent lighting in the school but felt that he could not admit this fact to his parents or teachers. It is well known that flickering lights can induce epileptic attacks, although usually fluorescent lights flicker with too high a frequency for this effect to occur. I quote this example as an indication of private, but very real, fears young people may have.

Probably the main cause of truancy is that the students have entered a cycle of learned helplessness. They are not doing very well academically and feel discouraged so 'bunk off' in order to escape criticism. In so doing they miss lessons and are likely to fall further behind. By not attending school they miss the humiliation and boys might even gain status among peers by their demonstration of independence from authority. There is a major gender difference, with low-achieving girls being more likely to sit quietly in class, not disturbing anyone, and often not being noticed.

This non-attendance not only handicaps these boys academically but also exposes them to the temptations of anti-social behaviour. If they hang around the amusement arcades and cafes they need money. This need, accompanied by a sense of boredom, leads to criminal activity, both for financial gain and for the excitement of the activity. Given these circumstances it is not surprising that we find that poor school attendance is the best predictor among young people of later criminal behaviour. The National Association for the Care and Resettlement of Offenders found that about 95 per cent of young men serving time in young offenders institutions had a history of truancy or exclusion from school. Of course, other variables were involved and about a third came from families who included members with some criminal background, but the school history contains the clearest warning.

Not everyone who misses school does so of their own accord and increasingly pupils are being excluded by schools. Between 1990–1 and 1994–5 exclusions went up from under 3,000 to over 12,000. Some exclusions are for a limited time scale, but in 1996–7 10,463 secondary students and 1,657 primary school pupils were permanently excluded, and boys made up 83 per cent of the total. Clearly some students can be so damaging to a school that their presence cannot be reasonably tolerated, but the trend for ever more exclusions might cause us concern. The motivation for this increase largely echoes that discussed earlier in relation to Statementing. By the process of exclusion, schools remove the more troublesome students from their roll and in so doing their average performance will be seen to be better.

Not only are boys in a clear majority among the excluded but there is also an ethnic imbalance with overall boys of Caribbean origin being four times more likely to be excluded than white boys and in some areas the ratio is even higher, e.g. Caribbean boys are seven times more likely to be excluded in the Borough of Islington.

If some effective, alternative provision was made for these young people then there might be less cause for concern, but in practice they join the truants in being on the streets, largely unsupervised, subject to temptation and exploitation. Their academic progress is likely to cease and they enter adulthood unskilled and often lacking the discipline and sense of routine to attend a workplace on a regular basis.

Clearly we do not know what to do with the troublesome youngsters and official policy in recent decades has oscillated between a belief in youth detention to provide a 'short, sharp, shock', and greater leniency in order to avoid the damaging effects of detention. From my limited experience of working within such a centre I found much to cause disquiet. Although staff maintained control for most of the day, in many respects it was the toughest boys who commanded the most fear and set the tone of the institution. All the worst elements of male peer groups, the competition and bullying, were evident. Examples of extreme sadism, ranging from savage assault to rape, were not uncommon. The toughest boys enjoyed their elevated status and manipulating their peers was for them a game. Others coped by keeping a low profile and attempting to appease the bullies. Some were totally bewildered and depressed by their experiences, seemingly not having the social skills to gain the support of others. Suicide is always a risk in these institutions. Whatever the best way of handling these youngsters may be, I am not certain that the all-male peer group of other delinquents provides the best environment for improvement.

10 Understanding the Boys

Young people today find themselves in a world which offers enormous opportunities, accompanied by as many uncertainties. No previous generation had such a stimulating environment, with access to an expanded system of further and higher education, cheap travel around the world, a vast range of television programmes, computer games and the Internet. Overall the population has become more prosperous and part of this wealth has reached many young people. At the same time life has become more difficult in various ways. The deterioration in public transport means that people are cut off from social life unless they own a car. The poorest in the community have become worse off in relative terms, and even for some in absolute terms. The changes in the benefit system have particularly affected those aged between 16 and 18. Contemporary consumerist values exaggerate the tensions, for being without the right clothes, or being unable to afford to go the popular 'rave', brings a sense of social exclusion.

The loss of jobs in the traditional male industries, such as mining and engineering, has removed one common path from school to work. In essence society for nearly two centuries offered a Faustian contract to men. They would be rewarded by income and status if they committed themselves to arduous and dangerous labour. In order to survive these demands, men sustained themselves through pride in their ability to cope and in their ability to distance themselves from their own bodies. Some pain or injury were seen as the inevitable price of survival. A macho culture was valued, in which control was essential and emotional expression was suppressed. The Faustian note was struck by the fact that these men had to deny essential parts of themselves, almost like selling their soul. What has now happened is that the contract has been broken. High salaries and high status are no longer guaranteed. Given this situation the obvious tactic is to withdraw from the other side of contract and be entrepreneurial in seeking the opportunities which are on offer, but the male culture has been slow to change, so that young men are encouraged to pursue goals which no longer can be realized. Clearly this description does not apply to all, and, as noted earlier, social and geographical variation is immense. Nevertheless, the change has been sufficiently extensive to undermine confidence, and create uncertainty, so that many young men see themselves being redundant, in all the aspects of that term.

At the same time the breakdown in family life has created another source of uncertainty, with the evidence being that boys suffer more than girls from this experience. It seems that girls and women are more able to set up informal networks of friends with whom they can talk freely about their problems, which allows them to cope with their life. The macho image of men being self-sufficient and autonomous, prevents male friendships from performing this role. Boys within single parent families, in a culture in which organized activities such as the Boy Scouts have declined, may be cut off from adult males and have to rely solely on their peer group for information and discussion. Neither the content nor the tone of the discourse in these groups help the members address their problems effectively.

Although outwardly young men may appear confident and cool, many achieve that appearance by postponing crucial decisions about careers and lifestyles, enjoying an extended adolescence as they drink their lager and cheer their football teams. Underneath this facade confusion may reign.

It is clear from this summary of the situation that remedial actions have to be aimed both at individuals and at the peer groups. Little can be done to change the social milieu in which young people find themselves, at least in the short term, so the main part of the complex which is open to change is in the way boys perceive and react to their circumstances. Essentially it is a mental act which is required, of reflection leading to appropriate action. Such mental processes can only occur in the minds of individuals, so the task is to address them directly. However, we know that the peer group has immense influence and if we can improve the discourse within the group, helping the young people to look forward, then that will also matter. We might then overcome the present situation in which many boys go along with their peers in resisting all aspects of school life, including academic learning, and then spend years in regret as they realize that they have denied themselves worthwhile career opportunities.

Psychological maturity requires making informed decisions. The first need for the young, therefore, is information, so that they can learn what, for example, the entry requirements are for a particular job, what the work involves, and what the rewards might be. The second requirement is to create a discussion, between people and also within the mind, so that options can be compared and consequences recognized. It is necessary to have self-knowledge, of one's own strengths, abilities, interests and temperament. The individual has to have the maturity to recognize weaknesses without losing confidence in the ability to achieve worthwhile outcomes. These processes of providing information and stimulating thought, need input from adults. For those aged up to 16, schools ought to make a major provision, after that age there is something of a vacuum. If we have to depend on schools providing enough to last the young men through to adulthood, then the programme of work will need extension. To inform and promote reflexivity, leading to the young acquiring a sense of agency, so that they can make realistic choices, is an ambitious agenda. It is, however, what we have to do, and the starting point for such a process must be in our understanding of the boys.

Recommended Reading

Part I: More Academic Books

Askew, S. and Ross, C. (1988) *Boys Don't Cry: Boys and Sexism in Education*, Milton Keynes, Open University Press.

Based on work done under the former ILEA in Hackney. Even now it provides a very good introduction to the issues.

Brod, H. and Kaufman, M. (ed.) (1994) *Theorizing Masculinity*, Thousand Oaks, CA, Sage.

An advanced text with a good collection of chapters by leading experts.

Chodorow, N. (1978) *The Reproduction of Mothering*, Berkeley, University of California Press.

It may seem odd to include a book on female development here, but it does cover the differences young boys and girls experience in being brought up, and how these differences socialize them into different adult roles.

Edley, N. and Wetherell, M. (1995) *Men in Perspective: Practice, Power and Identity*, Hemel Hempstead, Prentice-Hall/Harvester Wheatsheaf.

A very good introduction to the biological, psychological and social factors.

Head, J. (1997) *Working with Adolescents: Constructing Identity*, London, Falmer Press.

This book is meant to bridge the gap between theory and practice, introducing teachers and allied workers to ideas which might inform their professional practice.

Kilmartin, C.T. (1994) *The Masculine Self*, New York, Macmillan.

One of the few books which provides an introduction to the psychological issues.

Mac an Ghaill, M. (1994) *The Making of Men: Masculinities, Sexualities and Schooling*, Milton Keynes, Open University Press.

A mix of some tough sociological theory and reports on field work carried out in a secondary school.

Millard, E. (1997) *Differently Literate: Boys, Girls and the Schooling of Literacy*, London, Falmer Press.

The most comprehensive review of boys and literacy, covering media such as television, as well as reading and writing.

Part II: Books Related to School Practices

Bleach, K. (ed.) (1998) *Raising Boys' Achievement in Schools*, Stoke-on-Trent, Trentham Books.
A very varied set of contributions, but contains some useful material.

Bradford, W. (1997) *Raising Boys' Achievement*, Huddersfield, Kirklees Advisory Service.
A pioneering work, contains some useful tips for teachers.

Davidson, N. (1997) *Boys Will Be ... ?: Sex Education and Young Men*, London, Working with Men.
This book contains lesson plans and reports how the lessons actually went.

EOC/OFSTED (1996) *The Gender Divide: Performance Differences Between Boys and Girls at School*, London, HMSO.
A brief review of the situation in schools, with a list of questions about what can be done, to which readers are invited to respond.

Epstein, D., Elwood, J., Hey, V. and Maw, J. (eds) (1998) *Failing Boys? Issues in Gender and Achievement*, Milton Keynes, Open University Press.
Good on the background, why public concern has arisen recently, but provides little help in dealing with the issues.

Francis, P. (1996) *Boys Will Be Men*, Shropshire Education Services.
A mix of PSHE assignments developed in one school.

Lloyd, T. (ed.) (1997) *Let's Get Changed Lads: Developing Work with Boys and Young Men*, London, Working with Men.
A collection of about a dozen activities of the PSHE type, drawn from schools, family planning clinics, etc.

QCA (1997) *Can Do Better: Raising Boys' Achievement in English*, Hayes, Middlesex, QCA.

Salisbury, J. and Jackson, D. (1996) *Challenging Macho Values: Practical Ways of Working with Adolescent Boys*, London, Falmer Press.
This text contains a wealth of practical suggestions for work in schools on such diverse issues as bullying, sexual behaviour and harassment, language use, sport and the notion of an ideal male body. Teachers may wish to modify some of the plans, to adapt them to their own circumstances, but the bank of ideas provides a good starting point for planning 'boyswork'.

Bibliography

Abbott, F. (1990) *Men and Intimacy: Personal Accounts Explaining the Dilemmas of Modern Male Sexuality*, Freedom, CA, Crossing Press.

Adey, P.S., Shayer, M. and Yates, C. (1995) *Thinking Science*, London, Nelson.

Aggleton, P. (1987) *Rebels Without a Cause? Middle Class Youth, and the Transition from School to Work*, Lewes, Falmer Press.

Ahmad, Y. and Smith, P.K. (1994) 'Bullying in schools and the issue of sex differences', in J. Archer (ed.) *Male Violence*, London, Routledge.

Apter, T. (1989) *Altered Loves: Mothers and Daughters during Adolescence*, Hemel Hempstead, Harvester Wheatsheaf.

Arcana, J. (1983) *Every Mother's Son: The Role of the Mother in the Making of Men*, London, The Women's Press.

Archer, J. (ed.) (1994) *Male Violence*, London, Routledge.

Arnot, M. (1984) 'How shall we educate our sons?', in R. Deem, *Coeducation Reconsidered*, Milton Keynes, Open University Press.

Askew, S. and Ross, C. (1988) *Boys Don't Cry: Boys and Sexism in Education*, Milton Keynes, Open University Press.

Ausubel, D.P. (1968) *Educational Psychology: A Cognitive View*, New York, Holt, Rinehart and Winston.

Banks, M., Bates, I., Breakwell, G., Bynner, J., Emler, N., Jamieson, L. and Roberts, K. (1992) *Careers and Identities*, Milton Keynes, Open University Press.

Barber, C. (1996) 'The integration of a very able pupil with Asperger Syndrome into a mainstream school', *British Journal of Special Education*, 23, 1, 19–33.

Bell, N.J. and Bell, R.W. (eds) (1993) *Adolescent Risk Taking*, Newbury Park, CA, Sage.

Bem, S.L. (1975) 'Sex-role adaptability: one consequence of psychological androgyny', *Journal of Personal and Social Psychology*, 31, 634–43.

Berenstein, F.H. (1995) *Lost Boys: Reflections on Psychoanalysis and Countertransference*, New York, Norton.

Bilkser, D. and Marcia, J.E. (1991) 'Adaptive regression and ego identity', *Journal of Adolescence*, 14, 75–84.

Bleach, K. (ed.) (1998) *Raising Boys' Achievement in Schools*, Stoke-on-Trent, Trentham Books.

Blos, P. (1962) *On Adolescence: A Psychoanalytic Interpretation*, New York, Collier-Macmillan.

Bly, R. (1990) *Iron John*, Reading, MA, Addison-Wesley.

Bly, R. (1996) *The Sibling Society*, London, Penguin.

Boaler, J. (1997a) *Experiencing School Mathematics: Teaching Styles, Sex and Setting*, Milton Keynes, Open University Press.

Boaler, J. (1997b) 'Reclaiming school mathematics for girls', *Gender and Education*, 9, 1, 285–305.

Boone, J.A. and Cadden, M. (eds) (1990) *Engendering Men: The Question of Male Feminist Criticism*, London, Routledge.

Bourne, E. (1978) 'The state of research on ego identity; a review and appraisal' parts 1 and 2, *Journal of Youth and Adolescence*, 7, 223–52, 371–92.

Bowlby, J. (1951) *Maternal Care and Mental Health*, Geneva, WHO.

Bradford, W. (1997) *Raising Boys' Achievement*, Huddersfield, Kirklees Advisory Service.

Brittan, A. (1989) *Masculinity and Power*, Oxford, Blackwell.

Brod, H. and Kaufman, M. (ed.) (1994) *Theorizing Masculinities*, Thousand Oaks, CA, Sage.

Burns, R. (1982) *Self-Concept Development and Education*, London, Holt, Rinehart and Winston.

Burton, L. (ed.) (1986) *Girls Into Maths Can Go*, Eastbourne, Holt, Rinehart and Winston.

Callaghan, W.J. (1971) 'Adolescent attitudes toward mathematics', *The Mathematics Teacher*, 64, 751–5.

Caplan, P.J. (1979) 'Erikson's concept of inner space; a data-based reevaluation', *American Journal of Orthopsychiatry*, 49, 100–8.

Carpenter, H. (1989) *The Brideshead Generation: Evelyn Waugh and his Generation*, London, Weidenfeld and Nicolson.

Central Statistical Office (1997) *Social Trends 27*, London, HMSO.

Central Statistical Office (1998) *Social Trends 28*, London, HMSO.

Charlesworh, W.R. and La Frenier, P. (1983) 'Dominance, friendship utilization and resource utilization in preschool children's groups', *Ethology and Sociobiology*, 4, 175–86.

Chodorow, N. (1978) *The Reproduction of Mothering: Psychoanalysis and the Sociology of Gender*, Berkeley, University of California Press.

Chodorow, N. (1994) *Femininities, Masculinities, Sexualities: Freud and Beyond*, London, Free Association Books.

Clarke, A.M. and Clarke, A.D.B. (1976) *Early Experience: Myth and Evidence*, London, Open Books.

Coffield, F., Borrill, C. and Marshall, S. (1986) *Growing Up at the Margins*, Milton Keynes, Open University Press.

Cohen, D. (1990) *Being a Man*, London, Routledge.

Coleman, J.C. (1974) *Relationships in Adolescence*, London, Routledge and Kegan Paul.

Coleman, J.C. and Hendry, L. (1990) *The Nature of Adolescence*, London, Routledge.

Connell, R.W. (1989) 'Cool guys, swats and wimps: the interplay of masculinity and education, *Oxford Review of Education*, 15, 3, 291–303.

Connell, R.W. (1989) *Masculinities*, Cambridge, Polity.

Cote, J.E. (1996) 'Sociological perspectives on identity formation: the culture identity link and identity capital', *Journal of Adolescence*, 19, 417–28.

Cotterell, J. (1996) *Social Networks and Social Influences in Adolescence*, London, Routledge.

Cullingford, C. and Morrison, J. (1995) 'Bullying as a formative influence: the relationship between the experience of school and criminality', British Educational Research Journal, 21, 547–60.

Culp, R.E., Crook, A.S. and Housley, P.C. (1983) 'A comparison of observed and reported adult–infant interactions: effects of perceived sex', *Sex Roles*, 9, 475–9.

Damasio, A.R. (1994) *Descartes' Error: Emotion, Reason and the Human Brain*, London, Macmillan.

Davidson, N. (1997) *Boys Will Be ...? Sex Education and Young Men*, London, Working with Men.

Davis, J. (1990) *Youth and the Condition of Britain: Images of Adolescent Conflict*, London, Athlone Press.

Deem, R. (ed.) (1984) *Coeducation Reconsidered*, Milton Keynes, Open University Press.

Department for Education and Employment (DfEE) (1997) *Statistics of Education: Public Examinations GCSE and GCE in England 1986*, London, HMSO.

Department of Education and Science (1978) *Special Educational Needs: Report of the Committee of Enquiry into the Education of Handicapped Children and Young People* (The Warnock Report), London, HMSO.

Department of Education and Science (1989) *Girls Learning Mathematics*, London, HMSO.

Donnellan, C. (ed.) (1998) *Bullying*, Cambridge, Independence.

Douglas, J.W.B. (1964) *The Home and the School: A Study of Ability and Attainment*, London, MacGibbon and Kee.

Dowrick, S. (1992) *Intimacy and Solitude*, London, The Women's Press.

Duncan, P.D., Ritter, P.L., Dornbusch, S.M., Gross, R.T. and Carlsmith, J.M. (1985) 'The effects of pubertal timing on body image, school behavior and deviance', *Journal of Youth and Adolescence*, 14, 3, 227–35.

Easlea, B. (1981) *Science and Sexual Oppression: Patriarchy's Confrontation with Women and Nature*, London, Weidenfeld and Nicolson.

Easlea, B. (1983) *Fathering the Unthinkable: Masculinity, Scientists and the Nuclear Arms Race*, London, Pluto Press.

Edley, N. and Wetherell, M. (1995) *Men in Perspective: Practice, Power and Identity*, Hemel Hempstead, Harvester Wheatsheaf.

Entwistle, N.J. and Wilson, J.D. (1977) *Degrees of Excellence: The Academic Achievement Game*, London, Hodder and Stoughton.

Epstein, D. and Johnson, R. (1998) *Schooling Sexualities*, Milton Keynes, Open University Press.

Epstein, D., Elwood, J., Hey, V. and Maw, J. (ed.) (1998) *Failing Boys? Issues in Gender and Achievement*, Milton Keynes, Open University Press.

EOC/OFSTED (1996) *The Gender Divide: Performance Differences Between Boys and Girls at School*, London, HMSO.

Erikson, E.H. (1950) *Childhood and Society*, New York, Norton.

Erikson, E.H. (1968) *Identity, Youth and Crisis*, New York, Norton.

Fairbairn, W.R.D. (1952) *Psychoanalytic Studies of the Personality*, London, Tavistock.

Faludi, S. (1992) *Backlash: The Undeclared War Against Women*, London, Chatto and Windus.

Farrell, W. (1994) *The Myth of Male Power: Why Men Are the Disposable Sex*, London, Fourth Estate.

Fisher, S. (1973) *Body Consciousness*, London, Calder and Boyars.

Forrest, S., Biddle, G. and Clift, S. (1997) *Talking About Homosexuality in the Secondary School*, Horsham, Aids Education and Research Trust.

Francis, P. (1994) *Boys Will Be Men*, Shrewsbury, Shropshire Education Services.

Frazer, J.G. (1922) *The Golden Bough*, London, Macmillan.

Frydenberg, E. and Lewis, R. (1991) 'Adolescent coping: the different ways in which boys and girls cope', *Journal of Adolescence*, 14, 119–33.

Fryer, D. and Ullah, P. (1987) *Unemployed People: Social and Psychological Perspectives*, Milton Keynes, Open University Press.

Gaddis, A. and Brooks-Gunn, J. (1985) 'The male experience of pubertal change', *Journal of Youth and Adolescence*, 14, 61–9.

Galinsky, M. D. and Fast, I. (1966) 'Vocational choices as a focus of the identity search', *Journal of Counselling Psychology*, 13, 89–92.

Galloway, D. (1990) *Pupil Welfare and Counselling: An Approach to Personal and Social Education Across the Curriculum*, Harlow, Longmans.

Gaotti, K.M., Kozberg, S.F. and Farmer, M.C. (1991) 'Gender and developmental differences in adolescents' conceptions of moral reasoning', *Journal of Youth and Adolescence*, 20, 13–30.

Gaylin, W. (1992) *The Male Ego*, New York, Viking.

Gergen, M.M. and Davis, S.N. (ed.) (1997) *Towards a New Psychology of Gender*, London, Routledge.

Gilbert, R. and Gilbert, P. (1998) *Masculinity Goes to School*, London, Routledge.

Gilligan, C. (1982) *In a Different Voice*, Cambridge, MA, Harvard University Press.

Gipps, C. and Murphy, P. (1994) *A Fair Test?: Assessment, Achievement and Equity*, Milton Keynes, Open University Press.

Goleman, D. (1996) *Emotional Intelligrence*, London, Bloomsbury.

Gomez, J. (1991) *Psychological and Psychiatric Problems in Men*, London, Routledge.

Gray, J. (1992) *Men Are from Mars, Women Are from Venus*, New York, Harper-Collins.

Greenson, R. (1968) 'Dis-identifying from mother: its special importance for the boy', *International Psychoanalytic Journal*, 49, 370–4.

Grogan, S. (1998) *Men, Women and Body Image*, London, Routledge.

Hagerman, R. and Sobesky, W. (1989) 'Psychopathology in fragile-x syndrome', *American Journal of Orthopsychiatry*, 59, 1, 142–52.

Harding, J. (ed.) (1986) *Perspectives on Gender and Science*, Lewes, Falmer Press.

Hargreaves, D. J. and Colley, A.M. (ed.) (1986) *The Psychology of Sex Roles*, London, Harper and Row.

Harland, K. (1997) *Young Men Talking: Voices from Belfast*, London, Working with Men.

Haste, H. (1993) *The Sexual Metaphor*, London, Harvester Wheatsheaf.

Head, J. (1980) 'A model to link personality characteristics to a preference for science', *European Journal of Science Education* 2, 295–300.

Head, J. (1985) *The Personal Response to Science*, Cambridge, Cambridge University Press.

Head, J. (1997) *Working with Adolescents*, London, Falmer Press.

Head, J. and Ramsden, J. (1990) 'Gender, psychological type and science', *International Journal of Science Education*, 12, 115–21.

Hearn, J. and Morgan, R. (1990) *Men, Masculinities and Social Theory*, London, Unwin Hyman.

Hickson, A. (1996) *The Poisoned Bowl: Sex and the Public School*, London, Duckworth.

Hill, F. (1995) 'The provision of HIV/AIDS education in English colleges of further education', *Research in Science Education*, 25, 231–8.

Hodgson, J.W. and Fischer, J.L. (1979) 'Sex differences in identity and intimacy development', *Journal of Youth and Adolescence*, 8, 37–50.

Holland, J., Ramazanoglu, C. and Sharpe, S. (1993) *Wimp or Gladiator: Contradictions in Acquiring Masculine Identity*, London, Tufnell Press.

Holland, J., Ramazanoglu, C., Sharpe, S. and Thomson, R. (1998) *The Male in the Head: Young People, Heterosexuality and Power*, London, Tufnell Press.

Holyfield, S. (1989) 'Girls and information technology', in J. Head (ed.) *Girls and Technology*, London, King's College Occasional Paper.

Hood, J.C. (1993) *Men, Work and Family*, Newbury Park, CA, Sage.

Horrocks, R. (1994) *Masculinity in Crisis: Myths, Fantasies and Realities*, New York, St Martin's Press.

Hudson, L. and Jacot, B. (1991) *The Way Men Think: Intellect, Intimacy and Imagination*, New Haven, CT, Yale University Press.

Hutt, C. (1979) 'Sex role differentiation in social development', in H. McGurk (ed.) *Issues in Childhood Social Development*, London, Methuen.

Hyde, J.S. (1981) 'How large are cognitive gender differences?', *American Psychologist*, 36, 8, 892–901.

Jackson, D. (1995) *Destroying the Baby in Themselves: Why Did Two Boys Kill James Bulger?*, Nottingham, Mushroom Publications.

Johnson, S. and Murphy, P. (1986) *Girls and Physics: Reflections on APU Survey Findings*, APU Occasional Paper 4, London, DES.

Jordan, E. (1995) 'Fighting boys and fantasy play: the construction of masculinity in the early years of school', *Gender and Education*, 7, 1, 69–85.

Josephs, R.A., Markus, H. and Taararod, R.W. (1992) 'Gender differences in the sources of self-esteem', *Journal of Personality and Social Psychology*, 63, 391–402.

Josselson, R., Greenberger, E. and McConochie, D. (1977) 'Phenomenological aspects of psychosocial maturity in adolescence, part 1: Boys; part 2: Girls', *Journal of Youth and Adolescence*, 6, 25–56, 145–68.

Kelly, A. (ed.) (1987) *Science for Girls?* Milton Keynes, Open University Press.

Kenway, J. (1995) 'Masculinities in schools: under siege, on the defensive and under reconstruction?', *Discourse*, 16, 1, 59–79.

Kenway, J. and Gough, A. (1998) 'Gender and science education in schools: a review "with attitude"', *Studies in Science Education*, 31, 1–30.

Kilmartin, C.T. (1994) *The Masculine Self*, New York, Macmillan.

Kimmel, M.S. (ed.) (1988) *Changing Men: New Research on Men and Masculinity*, Newbury Park, Sage.

Klein, M. (1932) *The Psychoanalysis of Children*, London, Hogarth Press.

Koestler, A. (1967) *The Ghost in the Machine*, London, Hutchinson.

Kohlberg, L. (1981) *Essays in Moral Development*, San Francisco, Harper Row.

Kroger, J. (1996) *Identity in Adolescence: The Balance Between Self and Other*, 2nd edn, London, Routledge.

Kubie, L.S. (1954) 'Some unsolved problems of a scientific career', *American Scientist*, 42, 104–12.

Kuhn, D., Nash, C.S. and Brucken, L. (1978) 'Sex role concepts of two- and three-year-olds', *Child Development*, 49, 495–7.

Lamke, L.K. (1992) 'Adjustment and sex role orientation in adolescence', *Journal of Youth and Adolescence*, 11, 247–59.

Lee, C. (1993) *Talking Tough: The Fight for Masculinity*, London, Arrow.

Lees, S. (1986) *Losing Out*, London, Hutchinson.

Lever, J. (1976) 'Sex differences in the games children play', *Social Problems*, 23, 478–87.

Lloyd, T. (1997) *'Let's Get Changed Lads': Developing Work with Boys and Young Men*, London, Working with Men.

Lynn, D.B. (1962) 'Sex-role and parental identification', *Child Development*, 33, 555–64.

Mac an Ghaill, M. (1994) *The Making of Men: Masculinities, Sexualities and Schooling*, Milton Keynes, Open University Press.

Mac an Ghaill, M. (ed.) (1996) *Understanding Masculinities: Social Relations and Cultural Arenas*, Milton Keynes, Open University Press.

Maccoby, E.E. and Jacklin, C.N. (1975) *The Psychology of Sex Differences*, Oxford, Oxford University Press.

Maccoby, E.E. and Jacklin, C.N. (1987) 'Gender segregation in childhood', in E.H. Reese (ed.) *Advances in Child Development and Behavior*, 20, New York, Academic Press.

McGuinness, D. (1985) *When Children Don't Learn: Understanding the Biology and Psychology of Learning Difficulties*, New York, Basic Books.

MacInnes, J. (1998) *The End of Masculinity: The Confusion of Sexual Genesis and Sexual Differences in Modern Society*, Milton Keynes, Open University Press.

Maguire, M. (1997) 'Lads, loafers and homeboys: young men in the labour market' (unpublished paper, given at the British Educational Research Association).

Mahony, P. (1985) *School for Boys*, Hutchinson, London.

Mahony, P. (1989) 'Sexual violence and mixed schools', in C. Jones and P. Mahony (eds) *Learning Our Lines: Sexuality and Social Control in Education*, London, The Women's Press.

Malz, D. and Borker, R. (1983) 'A cultural approach to male–female miscommunication', in J. Gumperz (ed.) *Language and Social Identity*, Cambridge, Cambridge University Press.

Marcia, J.E. (1966) 'Development and validation of ego-identity statuses', *Journal of Personality and Social Psychology*, 3, 551–8.

Marcia, J.E. (1976) 'Identity six years after: a follow-up study', *Journal of Youth and Adolescence*, 5, 145–59.

Martin, K.A. (1996) *Puberty, Sexuality and the Self: Girls and Boys at Adolescence*, New York, Routledge.

Maslow, A.H. (1966) *The Psychology of Science: A Reconnaissance*, New York, Harper Row.

Matteson, D.P. (1975) *Adolescence Today: Sex Roles and the Search for Identity*, Homewood, IL, Dorsey Press.

Mead, M. (1962) *Male and Female*, Harmondsworth, Penguin.

Measor, L. and Sykes, P.J. (1992) *Gender and Schools*, London, Cassell.

Measor, L., Tiffin, C. and Fry, K. (1996) 'Gender and sex education: a study of adolescent responses', *Gender and Education*, 8, 3, 275–88.

Mellor, S. (1989) 'Gender differences in identity formation as a function of self–other relationships', *Journal of Youth and Adolescence*, 18, 361–75.

Miedzian, M. (1992) *Boys Will be Boys: Breaking the Link Between Masculinity and Violence*, London, Virago.

Millard, E. (1997) *Differently Literate: Boys, Girls and the Schooling of Literacy*, London, Falmer Press.

Miller, P. McC. and Plant, T. (1996) 'Drinking, smoking and illicit drug use among 15- and 16-year-olds in the United Kingdom', *British Medical Journal*, 313, 394–7.

Mitroff, I., Jacob, T. and Moore, E.T. (1977) 'On the shoulders of the spouses of scientists', *Social Studies of Science*, 7, 303–27.

Moir, A. and Moir, B. (1998) *Why Men Don't Iron: The Real Science of Gender Studies*, London, HarperCollins.

Money, J. and Ehrhardt, A. (1972) *Man Woman, Boy Girl*, Baltimore, MD, Johns Hopkins University Press.

Money, J. (1980) 'Endocrine influences and psychosexual status spanning the life-cycle', in H.M. Van Praagh (ed.) *Handbook of Biological Psychiatry, Part III*, New York, Marcel Dekker.

Moore, S. and Rosenthal, D. (1993) *Sexuality in Adolescence*, London, Routledge.

Montemayor, R. (1994) 'The study of personal relationships during adolescence', in R. Montemayor, G.R. Adams, and T.P. Gullotta (eds) *Personal Relationships during Adolescence*, Thousand Oaks, CA, Sage.

Murphy, D.A., Rotheram-Borus, M.J. and Reid, H.M. (1998) 'Adolescent gender differences in HIV-related sexual risk acts: cognitive and social factors', *Journal of Adolescence*, 21, 197–200.

Murphy, P.F. (1980) 'Gender differences: implications for assessment and curriculum planning', paper given at the British Educational Association annual conference, Manchester.

Murphy, P.F. and Gipps, C.V. (1996) *Equity in the Classroom: Towards and Effective Pedagogy for Boys and Girls*, London, Falmer Press.

Murray, C. and Dawson, A. (1983) *Five Thousand Adolescents: Their Attitudes, Characteristics and Attainments*, Manchester, Manchester University Press.

Mussen, P.H. and Jones, M.C. (1957) 'Self-conception, motivation, and interpersonal attitudes of late- and early-maturing boys, *Child Development*, 28, 2, pp. 243–55.

Mynard, H. and Joseph, S. (1997) 'Bully/victim problems and their association with Eysenck personality dimensions in 8- to 13-year-olds', *British Journal of Educational Psychology*, 67, 51–4.

Nardi, P.M. (ed.) (1992) *Men's Friendships*, Newbury Park, CA, Sage.

Nayak, A. and Kehily, M.J. (1996) 'Playing it straight: masculinities, homophobia and schooling', *Journal of Gender Studies*, 5, 211–30.

Newburn, T. and Stanko, E.A. (ed.) (1994) *Just Doing Boys' Business: Men, Masculinities and Crime*, London, Routledge.

Office for National Statistics (1998) *Social Trends*, London, HMSO.

OFSTED (1993) *Boys and English*, London, HMSO.

Paechter, C. and Head, J. (1996a) 'Power and gender in the staffroom', *British Journal of Educational Psychology*, 22, 1, 57–69.

Paechter, C. and Head, J. (1996b) 'Gender, identity and the body: life in a marginal subject', *Gender and Education*, 8, 1, 21–9.

Paechter, C. (1998) *Educating the Other: Gender, Power and Schooling*, London, Falmer Press.

Parker, A. (1996a) 'The construction of masculinity within boys' physical education', *Gender and Education*, 8, 2, 141–57.

Parker, A. (1996b) 'Sporting masculinities: gender relations and the body', in M. Mac an Ghaill (ed.) *Understanding Masculinities*, Milton Keynes, Open University Press.

Parry, O. (1997) 'Schooling is fooling; why do Jamaican boys underachieve in schools? *Gender and Education*, 9, 2, 223–31.

Prendergast, S. (1992) *This Is the Time to Grow Up: Girls' Experience of Menstruation in School*, Cambridge, Centre for Family Research.

Punter, A. and Burchell, H. (1996) 'Gender issues in GCSE English assessment', *British Journal of Curriculum and Assessment*, 6, 2, 20–48.

QCA (1998) *Can Do Better: Raising Boys' Achievement in English*, London, QCA.

Rekers, G.A. and Yates, C.E. (1976) 'Sex-typed play in feminoid boys versus normal boys and girls', *Journal of Abnormal Child Psychology*, 4, 1–8.

Roe, A. (1952) *The Making of a Scientist*, New York, Dodd Mead.

Rose, R.M., Gordon, T.P. and Bernstein, I.S. (1972) 'Plasma testosterone levels in male rhesus monkeys: influences of sexual and social stimuli', *Science*, 178, 643–5.

Rutherford, J. (1992) *Men's Silences: Predicaments in Masculinity*, London, Routledge.

Rutter, M. (1972) *Maternal Deprivation Reassessed*, Harmondsworth, Penguin.

Rutter, M., Maughan, B., Mortimore, P. and Ouston, J. (1979) *Fifteen Thousand Hours: Secondary Schools and their Effects on Children*, Shepton Mallet, Open Books.

Salisbury, J. and Jackson, D. (1996) *Challenging Macho Values: Practical Ways of Working with Adolescent Boys*, London, Falmer Press.

Schofield, M. (1965) *The Sexual Behaviour of Young People*, London, Longmans.

Seidler, V. (1989) *Rediscovering Masculinity*, London, Routledge.

Selkow, P. (1984) *Assessing Sex Bias in Testing*, Westport, CT, Greenwood Press.

Sewell, T. (1998) 'Loose cannons: exploding the myth of the "black macho" lad', in Epstein, D., Elwood, J., Hey, V. and Maw, J. (eds) *Failing Boys?*, Milton Keynes, Open University Press.

Sharp, S. and Smith, P. (1994) *Tackling Bullying in Your School: A Practical Handbook*, London, Routledge.

Shaw, J. (1995) *Education, Gender and Anxiety*, London, Taylor & Francis.

Skelton, A. (1993) 'On becoming a male physical education teacher: the informal culture of the students and the construction of hegemonic masculinity', *Gender and Education*, 5, 3, 289–303.

Smith, C. and Lloyd, B.B. (1978) 'Maternal behaviour and perceived sex of infant', *Child Development*, 49, 1263–5.

Spear, M.G. (1989) 'Differences between the written work of boys and girls', *British Educational Research Journal*, 15, 3, 271–7.

Stanworth, M. (1983) *Gender and Schooling: A Study of Sexual Division in the Classroom*, London, Hutchinson.

Stoller, R. (1985) *Representations of Gender*, New Haven, CT, Yale University Press.

Stoller, R.J. and Herdt, G.H. (1982) 'The development of masculinity: a cross-cultural study', *Journal of the American Psychoanalytic Association*, 30, 29–59.

Suin, R.M., Edie, C.A., Nicoletti, J. and Spinelli, P.R. (1972) 'The MARS: a measure of mathematics anxiety psychometric data', *Journal of Clinical Psychology*, 28, 373–5.

Super, P.E. (1957) *The Psychology of Careers*, New York, Harper Row.

Tacey, D.J. (1997) *Remaking Men: Jung, Spirituality and Social Change*, London, Routedge.

Tannen, D. (1991) *You Just Don't Understand: Women and Men in Conversation*, London, Virago.

Tattum, D. and Herbert, G. (1993) *Countering Bullying: Initiatives by Schools and Local Authorities*, Stoke-on-Trent, Trentham Books.

Terman, L.M. (1955) 'Are scientists different?', *Scientific American*, 192, 25–9.

Thorne, B. (1992) *Gender Play: Girls and Boys in School*, Milton Keynes, Open University Press.

Travis, C. and Wade, C. (1984) *The Longest War: Sex Differences in Perspective*, San Diego, Harcourt, Brace, Jovanovich.

Trenchard, L. and Warren, H. (1984) *Something to Tell You*, London, Gay Teenager's Group.

Vygotsky, L.S. (1962) *Thought and Language*, New York, Wiley.

Waterman, C.K. and Nevid, J.S. (1977) 'Sex differences in the resolution of the identity crisis', *Journal of Youth and Adolescence*, 6, 337–42.

Watkins, P. (1993) *Stand Before Your Bed*, London, Faber and Faber.

Weiner, G. and Arnot, M. (eds) (1987) *Gender Under Scrutiny: New Inquiries in Education*, London, Unwin Hyman.

Wellings, K., Field, J., Johnson, A.M. and Wadsworth, J. (1994) *Sexual Behaviour in Britain: The National Survey of Sexual Attitudes and Life Styles*, London, Penguin.

West, A., Noden, P., Edge, A. and David, M. (1998) 'Parental involvement in education in and out of school', *British Educational Research Journal*, 24, 4, 461–84.

Whyld, J. (1986) *Anti-Sexist Teaching with Boys*, Caistor, Whyld Publishing Co-op.

Williams, H. and Maloney, S. (1998) 'Well-meant, but failing on almost all counts: the case against statementing', *British Journal of Special Education*, 25, 1, 16–21.

Willis, P. (1977) *Learning to Labour: How Working-Class Kids Get Working-Class Jobs*, Aldershot, Gower.

Willottt, S. and Griffin, C. (1996) 'Men, masculinity and the challenge of long-term unemployment', in M. Mac an Ghaill (ed.) *Understanding Masculinities*, Milton Keynes, Open University Press.

Willmott, P. (1969) *Adolescent Boys in the East End of London*, Harmondsworth, Penguin.

Winefield, A.H., Tiggemann, M., Winefield, H.R. and Goldney, R.D. (1993) *Growing Up with Unemployment: A Longitudinal Study of its Psychological Impact*, London, Routledge.

Winnicott, D.W. (1958) *Collected Papers: Through Paediatrics to Pscho-Analysis*, London, Tavistock.

Winnicott, D.W. (1986) *Home is Where We Start From*, Harmondsworth, Penguin.

Wolff, S. (1993) *Loners: The Life Paths of Unusual Children*, London, Routledge.

Youniss, J., McClellan, J.A. and Strouse, D. (1994) 'We're popular, but we're not snobs', in R. Montemayor, G.R. Adams and T.P. Gullotta (eds) *Personal Relationships During Adolescence*, Thousand Oaks, CA, Sage.

Zigler, R.L. (1998) 'The four dimensions of moral education: the contribution of Dewey, Alexander and Goleman to a comprehensive taxonomy', *Journal of Moral Education*, 27, 1, 19–34.

Index